IT'S ALL IN YOUR
MIND

A Christian Perspective on Right and Wrong Thinking

Dr. Thomas Garrott Benjamin Jr.

It's All In Your Mind: A Christian Perspective on Right and Wrong Thinking

All Scripture quotations are taken from the King James Version or The Message Bible: New Testament With Psalms and Proverbs by Eugene H. Peterson. Copyright © 1993, 1994, 1995, by Eugene H. Peterson, NavPress, P.O. Box 35001, Colorado Springs, Colorado 80935.

Direct quotations from the Bible appear in italics.

ISBN: 1-4196-9870-2
ISBN-13: 9781419698705

Visit www.booksurge.com to order additional copies.

Published by Vision International Publishing
P.O. Box 781344
Indianapolis, IN 46278

Table Of Contents

This book is dedicated to my first grandchild,
Channing Carlyle Benjamin Jr.,
who is the joy of my life.

*The eyes of the future are looking back at
us and they are praying for us to see
beyond our time.*

– Terry Tempest Williams

About the Author

Tom Benjamin, Senior Pastor of the historic Light of the World Christian Church (Disciples of Christ), Indianapolis, Indiana, celebrated **38 years** as the Senior Pastor as well as his **41st year** in ministry in **October, 2007**. With this significant milestone, Bishop Benjamin has the longest pastorate of any Senior Pastor in the history of LWCC. He is also only the fourth **Senior Pastor** in the **141-year** history of the church. He is known widely for his commitment to excellence as a pastor and life coach and is widely known for his gifts of hospitality and generosity.

Bishop Benjamin's ministry has produced 33 seminary graduates with M.Div. degrees, five of that number have earned doctorates and four are on the doctoral track. They serve the church globally and ecumenically. They are one-third female and range from local pastors and chaplains to seminary administrators and denominational department heads. They serve mostly Disciples of Christ but also United Methodist and Southern Baptist congregations.

Their involvement ranges from being the first African American Dean of Students of the University of Chicago Divinity School, to being the first African American female pastor of a white Indiana Disciples of Christ congregation, the first African American Disciple to be the associate pastor of the largest United Methodist church in Indiana, the Christian Education Department executive for the Disciples of Christ, and the Chaplain of the Robin Run Senior Living facility of Indianapolis. This collectively is one of the unique, unparalleled and unprecedented contributions of Dr. Benjamin to the whole church and both confirm and help us understand his calling as Bishop. He was consecrated to the bishopric by an ecumenical group of national bishops in 1996 at the Indiana Convention Center.

He earned his undergraduate degree from St. Louis University (B.A.), and he also holds two earned cum laude graduate degrees (M.Div. and D.Min.) from Christian Theological Seminary, Indianapolis, Indiana. Additionally, he holds six honorary doctorate degrees and a host of other awards that recognize his deep commitment to quality preparation for ministers, as well as his bridge building between races and denominations in the city of Indianapolis.

Bishop Benjamin is a lifetime member of the NAACP. He is the founder of Project Impact Indianapolis, an intervention and counseling program for court-referred teens. It is a vital part of the community and is staffed by many members and ministers of LWCC church. He has conducted the longest running television and radio ministry in the city of Indianapolis.

In "Indy" he is called the "City's Pastor." And the August issue of *Indianapolis Monthly Magazine,* in 2007, named

Bishop Benjamin one of "Indy's most powerful." He is a community activist, in the best sense of the Word, as he consistently and courageously speaks truth to power. Dr. Benjamin has also raised millions of dollars in the Indianapolis community solely for the purpose of saving children, youth and families.

Nationally known for his standard of excellence in ministry, Pastor Benjamin was selected by **Morehouse College in Atlanta** as one of the recipients of its Distinguished Preacher's Award. He has also been the past National President of the Black Disciples Ministers' Fellowship.

Dr. Benjamin has been humbled to receive the Sagamore of the Wabash twice from two different Indiana governors. This designation is the highest honor that the governor bestows for distinguished service.

A pioneer in religious programming from the African American church, Dr. Benjamin shared his message across the world in the early '90s on BET, TBN and the Armed Forces Network. In January 2008, Dr. Benjamin was selected to present his teaching/preaching every day on the worldwide Internet ministry of GodTube.com. He joins his friend, Dr. Robert Schuller, Dr. Charles Stanley and others in spreading the Gospel worldwide 24 hours a day and 7 days a week.

Dr. Benjamin's passion is children, and he has authored four books: **Boys To Men, The Home Alone Syndrome,**

Mama's Boy, and his most recent book, *It's All In Your Mind.* He is an international speaker and life coach.

Bishop is an avid golfer as well as a music enthusiast. His pride is his family, consisting of his beautiful and creative life partner, Lady Beverly, three awesome adult sons, one darling daughter-in-law, and one *"grand"* grandson, Channing Carlyle, Jr.

Note: Light of the World Christian Church is the second oldest African American congregation in Indianapolis, founded in 1866. It now sits on a sprawling 40-acre campus with something to offer all of God's children from the cradle to the grave. It is noted as one of the most beautiful church sites in Indianapolis and is strategically located on the highest point in the city. It is truly a "City on a Hill" giving light and love to the whole community.

Acknowledgments

First, I want to thank the Lord Jesus for saving my soul and making me whole. Then I want to thank my grandmother, Marilla Roberts Jackson, for picking up the broken pieces of my life and miraculously molding them into God's original design. She prepared my heart and mind for Jesus to use my life. She even chose my wife, Beverly, who sweetens both my character and my coffee.

I would be remiss if I did not thank all who have touched my life and particularly my loving and supportive congregation, Light of the World Christian Church, for sharing and caring enough to allow me to write this book.

The core themes in this book were derived from a series of sermons that I gave in 2007 called "Right and Wrong Thinking." The biblical scripture notations were taken from the King James Version of the Bible, and from "The Message," a paraphrased translation by Eugene H. Peterson. This introduction notes biblical scripture from the New King James Version. Emphasis, where it is added, is mine.

I want to thank James L. Patterson, my editor and friend. He gave me invaluable assistance in preparing my sermon manuscripts for book publication.

I am grateful to my congregation who wholeheartedly supported the idea of the book, my loyal secretary Alice Hord, and to my friend Harmony Hines, one of the faithful volunteers in our congregation who spent countless hours typing the manuscript. God bless you all, and may your contributions help *to encourage folk to think about what they think about.*

Introduction

One day a member of my congregation asked me a very poignant question. She wanted to know why there was so much meanness, mayhem and murder in the world. At first I was tempted to answer her with my grandmother's simplistic but true biblical observation, "Sin is the cause of it all." The definition of sin, I later learned in seminary, was rebellion against God. It is the war between the flesh (self) and the Spirit (God). The sin battle is a never ending battle. The battle is constant but in order for us to win, we have to change the way we think. Because once sin takes control of our minds, our bodies will follow. The battle is won or lost in the mind. Whether it is losing weight or staying out of jail, or getting rid of a bad habit, it does not matter what the issue is, I contend that the resolution of that issue is all in our minds. It is not what happens to us. It is our attitude towards what happens to us that makes the difference. However, my answer to the member was the beginning of a deeper inquiry into her question. I remember saying to her I have come to the conclusion that all of our actions, whether negative or positive, come as a result of the way we think. I indicated that there is such a thing as right thinking and wrong thinking. Right thinking produces right results and wrong thinking produces wrong results.

We are living in a time where for many a sense of right and wrong is unclear. You may be asking yourself what determines right and wrong thinking. What constitutes right and wrong can be debated *ad infinitum*. I based all of the chapters in this book on the truth of God in the Bible and the wisdom of the ages that lines up with that truth. I find no profit in debating this issue subjectively. Whether the reader agrees or not, I have used an objective standard as a basis from which to launch my conclusions. I believe in God as the First Cause for everything. The first book of the Bible says it best: "In the beginning God created..." That means that our minds came from God. Our ability to think comes from God. Yet because God gives us free will the choice is ours as to how we think and what we think. People are not born thinking right. They are not even reborn thinking right. You are not baptized into thinking right. You do not think right just because you are a Christian, a Muslim or a Buddhist. People do not automatically think right, so it should follow that they cannot automatically act right. We must be taught to think right. We must be trained to think right. Every child needs a standard and a model of right thinking. My grandmother taught me that standard is the truth of the Word of God as expressed in the person of Jesus of Nazareth. Right thinking is synonymous with the mind of Christ.

There are four scriptures that I believe best represent the mind of Christ and form the bedrock of my thinking on this issue. Proverbs 23:7 says as a man *thinks in his heart, so is he* (NKJV). Romans 12:2 says *do not be conformed to this world, but be transformed by the renewing of your mind, that you may prove what is that good and acceptable and perfect will of God* (NKJV). Philippians 2:5 says *let this mind be in you which was also in Christ Jesus* (NKJV). Philippians 4:8-9 says: *Summing it all up, friends, I'd say you'll do best by filling your minds and meditating on things true, noble, reputable, authentic, compelling, gracious—the best, not the worst; the beautiful, not the ugly; things to praise, not things to curse. Put into practice what you learned from me, what you heard and saw and realized. Do that, and God, who makes everything work together, will work you into his most excellent harmonies.*

In the face of the American moral decline, I feel it necessary to raise this issue of right and wrong thinking. We keep analyzing the symptoms and ignoring the cause. What makes a man purposely fly a plane into a building? Wrong thinking. What makes a person break into a classroom with a high-powered rifle or handgun trying to kill everyone in sight? Wrong thinking. What makes a young man rape and murder a promising college student he never met? Wrong thinking. What makes a public official destroy his career and the trust of his family by sexual scandal? Wrong thinking. You say that all of these examples are forms of insanity. Whatever you call it by any other name it is still wrong thinking.

It seems that we continue to go around in circles to try and discover the cause of our corruption. In the orthodox

Christian tradition, we would be compelled to agree with my late grandmother that sin or our separation from God has resulted in our ethical and moral bankruptcy. In this era or "error," it is overwhelming to think that there is so much justification for wrong thinking. The black community is a microcosm of what has become an American tragedy. In far too many of our states, we have more young men in prison than we do in college. It is daunting to think that the United States Department of Justice predicts that 32% of black males will enter state or federal prison during their lifetimes. Among the black population, eight out of 10 children are born to unwed mothers. Fatherlessness has become epidemic and pandemic in our country. The divorce rate is now tipping the scale to where there are more divorces than marriages. We are using taxpayers' hard earned money to fight an immoral and unethical war. We are seeing our courts being clogged over the issues of abortion and same-sex marriage. The blood of our children runs in the streets of our cities. Homicide, suicide and genocide have become all too commonplace on the human landscape. Surely sin is at the core of all of this, but I have come to the conclusion that this same sin first takes control of the mind. Sinful thinking is wrong thinking because it separates man from God and from living out the true nature of his being, which is love. When we think right, we think about how to help. When we think wrong, we think about how to hurt. It is really as simple as that.

So these pages are dedicated to what I consider to be one of the most obvious but overlooked determinants of our disorder. Simply stated, it is that what we think about is what we bring about. The Bible sums it up in one succinct statement in Proverbs 23:7, as a man *thinks in his heart, so is he...* (NKJV). As I read that passage over and over, it became clear to me that much of our sadness and madness is inextricably connected to the way in which we think. In other words, "It's all in your mind." I chose this phrase as a title because I could not find any title that better represents the biblical truth that basically we are what we think we are. I, in no way, want to discount the deep theological issues of sin, salvation, regeneration, justification and sanctification. There have been tons of books and articles written about these subjects. However, seldom do we see a Christian perspective on right and wrong thinking. This in no way represents an exhaustive or even erudite examination of all the issues and sub-issues that this book raises. It is just one pilgrim pastor's attempt to understand the nature of our demise as a people.

I would also say that we owe it to future generations, our children and our grandchildren, to teach them how to think and ultimately to teach them the true difference between right and wrong as based on the Bible and the Word of God. The battlefield is the mind. It is an issue of control. Either God or the enemies of God will rule the mind. There will be no middle ground. There is no place for two rulers. God and the truth of God will rule the mind or the devil and all of his demons will rule the mind. We have to start early and work while it is day in order to turn back the tide of chaos and corruption that has infected the body politic of this planet. We can save the planet by right thinking. We developed right thinking by lining our thoughts up with the truth of God in the Bible. Truth is love. Where love is in control there is no place for hate. These are the lessons that we must teach our children if mankind is to survive. I can safely say that we will rise or fall on how we think. The biblical prophet Hosea was right, when he said, "My people are destroyed for lack of knowledge." In other words, it's all in your mind.

Tom Benjamin
2008
Indianapolis, Indiana

Chapter 1
'As A Man Thinketh'

'My mind is my biggest asset. I expect to win every tournament I play.' – Tiger Woods

California is more than earthquakes, smog, wildfires and traffic gridlock. Despite the occasional natural disasters that Californians endure, it remains one of the most beautiful areas on earth. It is called the "Golden State" for good reason – plenty of sunshine. Earthquakes or not, about 36 million people called California home at the turn of the 21st century, according to the U.S. Census Bureau.

Our baggage included sunglasses and golf clubs when Beverly and I went there for Christmas 2007 to visit our children. Because we were looking forward to a period of refreshing, renewal and rest from my ministerial and administrative responsibilities, we were eager to reach our destination.

It was the first Christmas away from my congregation in 38 years. It was also the first time a Benjamin baby had been born in 32 years as my middle son, Channing, and my daughter-in-law, Claudia, were ready to deliver our first grandchild. My thoughts ran deep over the excitement raised by the prospect of a new grandson. The questions which these feelings posed were many.

How will he look? What special talents and abilities will God grace him with? Will he be a pastor or a professional golfer? Just as importantly, what kind of world will he be entering?

I do know this much. By God's grace, my new grandchild will come into a place that is quite different from the one I arrived in at St. Louis, Missouri, in 1942. For certain, we had our challenges to overcome back then. The problems in our urban and rural communities were many and complicated: segregation, educational deficiencies, and unemployment. My grandson, however, will face a new set of challenges. He will have to deal with drugs, greed and violence, which are inextricably bound to each other. They have a death grip on contemporary America. As a child of color, he will be tested by a unique set of social obstacles right off the bat. But he will learn, sometimes painstakingly, that the most effective remedy to the troubles he encounters is within him. He has been born into a society that has inherent factors that will test two things inside of him: the godly faith that he will receive from his parents and his resolve to overcome any adversity. By God's grace and proper parenting he will not only survive but thrive.

WE ARE WHAT WE THINK WE ARE

Of this I am certain: The mind is the key to unlocking our problems and possibilities. The wisdom that the prophet

Solomon shares on this point is power packed: *For as he thinketh in his heart, so is he…* (Proverbs 23:7). It is important to understand this statement because if there are persons that we admire, what we are really admiring are their thoughts. We tend to think we are admiring their success and their achievements, but what we really esteem most about them are their thoughts. We have the ability to tell what another person is thinking by what he says. What you say telegraphs what you are thinking. We don't need to be able to read a person's mind. The proverbial biblical phrase "as a man thinketh in his heart, so is he" was the *secret* long before Rhonda Byrne produced her controversial bombshell book *The Secret*.

The problems we have and the solutions to those problems are closely bound to our thinking. Our errant thought process has led us to pain, poverty, prison, and paralysis. Our mindset has a direct affect upon our health and wealth. It's literally all in our minds. Too many of us are unnecessarily sick and we die prematurely because of our mindset. Wrong thinking is our dilemma. Reversing this process will require a total reorganization and transformation of our thinking.

The apostle Paul said: *And be not conformed to this world: but be ye transformed by the renewing of your mind, that ye may prove what is that good, and acceptable, and perfect, will of God* (Romans 12:2).

I found this same truth in a book written by Englishman James Allen in the early 1900s. That book is titled *As A Man Thinketh*. Though it is only 70 pages, the book was a blessing that helped to shape my own thinking in my intellectually formative years. I could not stop reading it. It is one of the most important works that has ever been written. It can be downloaded free as an electronic book at www.asamanthinketh.net/download.htm. Come on folks, there are no excuses. Both the information and inspiration are available.

Allen was born in Leicester, England, in 1864. Not much is known about his early life, but he is believed to have worked for an English corporate executive as a personal secretary until 1902. When he "retired" at the age of 38, he moved with his wife to a small cottage in Ilfracombe, England, where he wrote more than 20 works before dying suddenly at the age of 48.

Allen proved that despite living a short life, a person can be as productive as he wants to be. "The aphorism, *As a man thinketh in his heart, so is he*, not only embraces the whole of man's being, but is so comprehensive as to reach out to every condition and circumstance of his life," wrote Allen. "A man is literally what he thinks, his character being the complete sum of all his thoughts."

There is hardly a more important factor in human development than *we are what we think*. This is among the most significant concepts that we can ever grasp. It can completely and literally revolutionize our lives. This fact has always been there. Now it is time for us to embrace it. Everything we want and need is caught up in our ability to grasp this truth. We have wants and needs, but at some point we must begin to think about what we think about. What we think about determines our character and ultimately controls our circumstances and destiny. Norman Vincent Peale said it this way: "Change your thoughts and you change your world." William James said, "The greatest discovery to my generation is that man can alter his life simply by altering his attitude of mind."

When we are sick, we have to learn to think health. When we are poor, we have to think plenty. The trick of the enemy is to get us to think the way he thinks. Conversely, the Holy Spirit is trying to get us to think the way He thinks. This is a classic and ongoing tug of war in our minds. It is called the inner conflict. The stakes are high in this constant battle – back and forth between the forces of good and evil – over who controls the mind. The mind is our Gettysburg, our Vietnam, our Jena, and our Baghdad. It is a conflict for control of our very soul. There is a story about a Navajo grandfather who once told his grandson, "Two wolves live inside me. One is the bad wolf, full of greed and laziness, full of anger and jealousy and regret. The other is the good wolf, full of joy and compassion and willingness and a great love for the world. All the time, these wolves are fighting inside me."

"But grandfather," the boy asked, "which wolf will win?"

The grandfather answered, "The one I feed."

There is hardly a more important factor in human development than *we are what we think*. This is among the most significant concepts we can ever grasp. It can completely and literally revolutionize our lives. This fact has always been there. Now it is time for us to embrace it. Everything we want and need is caught up in our ability to grasp this truth. We have wants and needs, but at some point we must begin to think about what we think about. What we think about determines our character and ultimately controls our circumstances and destiny.

What we think determines what we believe. What we believe determines who we are and what we can have. Once we achieve the victory in the inner conflict, or the mind, we have the victory in the outer conflict or life. We can say we have faith, but our faith will be amiss if we do not think right. Thought precedes faith. Everything, absolutely everything, begins with a thought. We can have anything that we can think about because if we think about something, it is already a reality because our thoughts are our reality. Those thoughts may take a while to manifest, but just hold on, they will.

Dr. R. G. Rush, pastor of Inspiring Body of Christ Church in Dallas, Texas, wrote in his book *May I Have Your Order, Please? How to get what you want from God*, that followers of Christ ought to become comfortable with abiding, or remaining in Him: "To abide in Christ is to renounce any independent life of our own, to give up trying to think our thoughts, or to cultivate our feelings, and to simply and constantly rely on Christ to think His thoughts in us and to form His purposes in us. Again, this is possible when you allow Christ, through the Holy Spirit, to direct every aspect of your life. The Apostle Paul put it very succinctly: *Let this mind be in you, which was also in Christ Jesus* (Philippians 2:5). How do we do this? People have to make every effort to get the Word of God into their spirit. It requires more than simply going to church on Sunday. A transformed mind comes by a daily conversation with God through His Word. In other words, daily personal Bible study, group Bible study, weekly Sunday school and those things which we often resist move from being optional to being mandatory.

Everything, absolutely everything, begins with a thought. We can have anything that we can think about because if we think about something, it is already a reality because our thoughts are our reality.

Those thoughts may take a while to manifest, but just hold on, they will.

SUCCESS IS FIRST A THOUGHT

What is today the multibillion-dollar corporation Microsoft was first a thought in Chairman Bill Gates' mind. Gates, who dropped out of Harvard University after two years, was ranked as the richest person in the world from 1995 to 2007, with estimates putting his net worth at $56 billion.

Likewise, Oprah Winfrey's Harpo Productions was first a thought. Born the daughter of a housemaid and a coal miner in an impoverished rural Mississippi family, Winfrey has become the world's only African-American billionaire and the first black woman billionaire in world history. She had amassed a fortune of more than $2.5 billion by 2008.

The late John H. Johnson's publishing empire, with its flagship publications *Ebony* and *Jet* magazines, was first a thought. Johnson, founder of the Johnson Publishing Company, was the first black person to appear on the Forbes 400 list of wealthiest persons. He started the Chicago, Illinois-based international media and cosmetics corporation beginning with a thought. The mega-company had accumulated a fortune of close to $500 million by the time of his death in 2005.

The athletic ability of LeBron James, the National Baskeball Association superstar, was first a thought. James thought, "I think I want to play basketball. I think I want to be the best at it." If you do not first think it, you will not get it. Jordin Sparks' musical career also began with a thought. Although she never had any formal vocal training, the Glendale, Arizona, resident fought back fierce competition to become the American Idol in 2007.

Whether it is the oratory and activism of a Martin Luther King Jr., or the brilliance and boldness of a Nelson Mandela or the sacred service of a Mother Teresa or the inspiring leadership of a Barak Obama, each of them began their work with a thought.

Light of the World Christian Church, the second oldest (1866) African-American congregation in Indianapolis, Indiana, began as a thought. It has now blossomed into 40-acre church complex. The T. Garrott Benjamin Jr. Senior Living Center located down the street from the church began as a thought. Because we have been a blessing to others, God continues to bless us. For example, our congregation forgave the quarter-of-a-million dollars debt of a smaller congregation, and before the ink was dry on the paper, God gave us a $5 million HUD grant to build the senior living center. You cannot beat God giving, and you cannot beat God thinking.

God works through what we think. You will give generously when you line your thoughts up with His Word. The late great Howard Thurman, my friend and mentor said: "When you and God become one, all of life's resources will flow toward you."

As a matter of a fact, our character comes from a thought. Our identity, reality and destiny all come from a thought. We can make the effort to renew our minds if we choose to do so. If our minds are new, if they are transformed, it is a done deal and everything else will follow. James Allen said, "As you think, you travel, and as you love, you attract. You are today where your thoughts have brought you; you will be tomorrow where your thoughts take you."

Our very existence, the fact that we are alive today is not just the result of an egg being fertilized in our mother's womb. It began with a thought. Our parents thought about each other, desired a baby (or perhaps not), acted on it and we are the result. The very essence of creation itself initially came from the mind of God.

THINK IT THEN SAY IT

The late great teacher, poet, songwriter and human rights advocate James Weldon Johnson said, "And God said, 'I think I'll make me a man.'" After God thought it, what did He do? He spoke it. We need to emulate God's pattern in our thinking. If the Holy Spirit puts a thought in our minds, we ought to say it. He has put some things in our hearts and on our minds, but we are not saying them because we are not really sure that what we think can become reality. It has been said, "What the mind can conceive, and what the heart believe, we can achieve because if it is on our minds, it might as well be in our hands."

I did not get where I am by *just* being educated or industrious, as important as those character traits may be. I got there by believing in a God who plants powerful thoughts in my mind. I mean monumental thoughts, prosperous thoughts, progressive thoughts, and achieving thoughts. It has never occurred to me that I should be anything but blessed. It has never occurred to me that I should be anything but favored. It has never occurred to me that I should have to beg or borrow but that I should be the lender! I should be on top not beneath. I should be the head and not the tail. This is the Word of God, will of God, and it supports my thesis that it is *all* in your mind.

'What the mind can conceive, and what the heart believe, we can achieve because if it is on our minds, it might as well be in our hands... It has never occurred to me that I should be anything but blessed. It has never occurred to me that I should be anything but favored. It has never occurred to me that I should have to beg or borrow but I should be the lender! I should be on top not beneath. I should be the head

and not the tail. This is the Word of God, will of God, and it supports my thesis that it is *all* in your mind.

Jesus said: *This mountain, for instance: Just say, 'Go jump in the lake' – no shuffling or shilly-shallying – and it's as good as done.* (Mark 11:23). Consider another thought for a moment. The home you are living in, no matter what kind of home it is, no matter how much it is worth, the first thing you did was think about it. When we think about something, it already is. The car you are driving, you thought about it first. We can talk to ourselves and speak whatever we desire into reality. Dr. Robert H. Schuller, my dear friend and mentor, said, "It takes but one positive thought when given a chance to survive and thrive to overpower an entire army of negative thoughts."

BELIEVE IT

Not only must we think and say what we want to achieve but the Bible says we must *believe* it, too. The Book of Matthew describes in Chapter 21:18-22 how Jesus, who was hungry at the time, cursed the fig tree that He came upon because it had no fruit. His disciples marveled at how soon the fig tree withered away and brought this up to Jesus. In response, Jesus reminded them of the power that they possessed – which He had imputed unto them – through merely what they said and believed.

All things whatsoever we shall ask in prayer, in our minds, in our hearts, whatever we ask believing it already is. It already exists. If it exists in our minds, it exists in the world. *We* must believe it. The ancient children of Israel spent 40 years, instead of the 40 days travel time it should have taken them, trying to enter the land promised to them, not because of unyielding border guards but because of their *unbelief*. The lesson that I am trying to impart to you is to believe what you declare and never doubt it. You have to speak the Word. But not only speak the Word, speak it positively and powerfully. You must understand that the issues of life come out of the heart and out of the mind. Solomon, who was the wisest man that ever lived, said, *Keep vigilant watch over your heart; that's where life starts* (Proverbs 4:23).

SPEAKING SPIRITS

When the Holy Spirit takes power over my mind, over my thoughts, over my speech, the anointing of God begins to flow. Whatever is happening in my life begins to come into order. Whatever pain I feel begins to dissipate. I begin to walk in my own speech. I become a speaking spirit, which is a phrase I picked up from fellow minister E. Bernard Jordan. I can say to my problems, or the problems I face, mountain be removed!

Dr. Schuller asserted a similar truth when he said, "Our greatest lack is not money for any undertaking, but rather ideas. If the ideas are good, cash will somehow flow to where it is needed."

Believe it or not, we can actually speak to any sickness that tries to take hold of our body. We can talk to our pain. We can speak to our grief and say, mountain be moved. That is what I love about Jesus. He is the Speaking Spirit. You can get the same mind that was in Jesus in you. This is exactly what the Bible means when it instructs us to renew our minds. When Jesus walked around places in his native Israel more than 2,000 years ago, He didn't just walk but He talked. When He spoke, things happened. That is why He always had crowds following Him everywhere He went. He spoke to a lame man and he began to walk. He spoke to a dead man and he rose up. He spoke to the people who followed Him and they lifted their eyes up. He spoke on Calvary and we all looked up. When He spoke something happened because He had the mind of God.

When you have the mind of God, you can do anything. Nothing shall be impossible to you because you are transformed from flesh to spirit. You can walk through difficulties, trials, troubles and they will not bother you. Jesus said have faith...*and nothing shall be impossible unto you* (Matthew 17:20).

James Allen wrote: "Man is made or unmade by himself. In the armory of thought he forges the weapons by which he destroys himself. He also fashions the tools with which he builds for himself heavenly mansions of joy and strength and peace."

The shepherd boy David and his countrymen faced their biggest opposition from the giant Goliath, who was a massive man by any stretch of the imagination. The biblical scripture says this enormous warrior was about 9 feet and 9 inches tall, and it described his coat alone as weighing 126 pounds (I Samuel 17:4-5). The soldiers of Israel looked at the giant and concluded that he was too big. They said something like, "He is too big we can't beat him." But David looked at the giant and said, "He's just the right size, I can't miss him."

We must come to the realization that we are a speaking spirit. When we think deliverance and speak it, we can expect deliverance. The same thing will happen when we think healing and speak it. It is also true for hope, prosperity, and anything else that we first think and then speak. Thinking right will compel us to believe right, which will in turn cause us to receive right. We are all made in the *Imago Dei* (the Image of God). Since we are made in His image, we ought to have the desire to be just like Him. That is, to think big thoughts. Is there a bigger thought than the universe? Just look at how massive the universe is that God created. We need to speak the things we want, and continue to believe what we spoke until it happens.

In the meantime, we should be careful not to fall for the devil's tricks. He is the personification of evil often referred to as the enemy. He would gladly trick us out of our inheritance, if we let him. If there are any people on the face of the earth who should be walking in godly prosperity, it should be the people of God. We are made in God's image, and there is nothing poor about God, except His concern for the poor. The biblical scripture says in 3 John 1:2, *Beloved, I wish above all things that thou mayest prosper and be in health, even as thy soul prospereth.*

If we embrace these principles, there is no way we can have dull hearing and clouded vision. It just cannot happen when we walk by faith and not by sight. The insight that has been presented in this chapter offers a key to the puzzles that many of us face daily. Namely, why is it that Christians are saved, but we cannot seem to move any higher in our lives than where we are? How can we be so blessed and yet so broke? How is it that we can be saved and we still not think right? We should be careful not to let the enemy deceive us into thinking that we are in right standing with God's salvation but it is still *OK* to live below our privileges. We can have chaos or conquest, depending on our thoughts.

Why is it that Christians are saved, but we cannot seem to move any higher in our lives than where we are? How can we be so blessed and yet so broke? How is it that we can be saved and we still not think right?

HATERS HALT

We know that our Father in heaven is the Creator of everything that is good and the sustainer of our lives. Keeping our thinking in line with His Word is difficult to accomplish without regularly practicing it through our behavior. But once we begin to do so, He will give us a clean heart and renew a right spirit within us. With a new spirit, we will shy away from the pitfalls of vanity and gossip, and the small talk that means nothing. Our words are so influential that choosing the wrong ones is bound to result in negative consequences. When we speak positive words, we will begin to cease our judgment of others. To judge another is, has always been, and always will be God's responsibility.

Too many of us have a case of low self-esteem brought on by a lack of knowledge of who we are and whose we are. We are little gods, according to the biblical scripture John 10:34. Since we are made in God's image, then we look like Him and should desire to act like Him. I teach my church to say aloud: *We are not God but we are like God. We are not God but we are made in His image.* The Psalmist says God made us a *little lower than the angels, and hast crowned us with glory and honor* (Psalm 8:5). God stands ready and willing to remove every ounce of envy and jealousy we have toward other people because such thoughts are a roadblock to right living. It is clear that He has given us life and given it abundantly. He has blessed us with a mind to think great thoughts, in fact enormous thoughts. He has also gifted the vast majority of us with a tongue, so we can speak what we think. Along with that, we have the power to declare through that tongue that we choose to take the path of victory in the battle of the mind. We can surely declare that the enemy is defeated and Jesus is exalted in our minds. This is the same mind through which we can have what we desire if we think it, believe it and say it. Too many of us have a case of low self-esteem brought on by a lack of knowledge of who we are and whose we are.

We are little gods, according to the biblical scripture John 10:34. Since we are made in God's image, then we look like Him and should desire to act like Him. I teach my church to say aloud: *We are not God but we are like God. We are not God but we are made in His image.* The Psalmist says God made us a *little lower than the angels, and hast crowned us with glory and honor* (Psalm 8:5).

Right thinking makes us realize that we need Him in order to be saved. Wrong thinking says that we can just go ahead, live our lives as we see fit and not be concerned about what is going to happen here or in the hereafter. But that seems to be quite a gamble to me. I don't want to miss heaven here or hereafter. Do you? Let's make our thoughts His thoughts and see if He won't open up the windows of heaven and pour us out a blessing that is so substantial we won't have room enough to receive it. When you get right down to it, *it's all in your mind.*

Chapter 2
A Message From The Trees

'Preach the Gospel and use words where necessary.' – Mother Teresa

No one is immune from the fact that we all grapple with life's triumphs and disappointments. People respond to the ups and downs of life often in very different ways. Some folks are not afraid to face their problems head on, while others seem to be constantly running away from them.

In the 1974 movie *The Autobiography of Miss Jane Pittman*, star actress Cicely Tyson played Jane Pittman. The life of her fictional character unfolded over more than a century. From slavery to the early 1960s, petite little Jane Pittman dealt with the many pressures she encountered by occasionally sitting next to an old oak tree and pouring out her problems. The film was based on a novel by Ernest J. Gaines, who was born on a Louisiana plantation in 1933. Set in rural southern Louisiana, Pittman's character went through enough hills and valleys in life to fill two books. Gaines described how he regularly sat on the front porch of his Louisiana home in "the Quarters," the servant living area, with adults who came to visit his Aunt Augusteen, the woman who cared for him and his siblings, and quietly listened to stories of his ancestors and the old days. Based on the culture that Jane Pittman lived in, it would not have been uncommon for her to have been talking to an oak tree. "Anybody caught talking to a chinaball tree or a thorn tree got to be crazy," she said in the movie. "But when you talk to an oak tree that's been here all these years, and knows more than you'll ever know, it's not craziness; it's just the nobility you respect."

Nobility indeed; oak is a symbol of strength and endurance. The oak tree is one of the world's strongest trees. When it grows in a forest or among a group of trees, it may reach as high as 60 to 100 feet, with a trunk ranging from 30 to 40 feet up, and a circumference that is commonly eight to 10 feet, though some old oak trees grow to seven times that large around. It is supported and anchored by its roots, which play a key role in the tree's life by absorbing water and minerals, storing energy for fuel, and producing the chemicals such as tannins and salicylic acid, which help to regulate the growth of other plants in its vicinity. Oak roots grow best where they can get the nutrients they need. That is, oxygen, water and minerals, without which the tree cannot bear fruit.

A tree's growth process is analogous to the human journey. Just as what kind of nourishment it receives determines the sort of fruit it bears, what goes on in the heart and mind of a man or woman will ultimately become evident in their lives. *If you grow a healthy tree, you'll pick healthy fruit. If you grow a diseased tree, you'll pick worm-eaten fruit. The fruit tells you about the tree* (Matthew

12:33). Generally speaking the taller the tree the deeper its roots. Some trees have been living hundreds of years and are still standing because of their root systems. The most severe hurricanes and tornadoes cannot knock them down while other trees fall easily under such pressure. This was illustrated in the aftermath of Hurricane Katrina and the storms and tornados that followed it, which changed the landscape of the South and Midwest. The quality of a tree's fruit is determined by how far down its taproot grows beneath ground, not by its limbs. The oak tree's root system runs two ways: shallow and deep. In the nature of things, the roots that run near the surface are delicate and extremely sensitive to sudden changes in pressure or in the grade of the soil. The surface root system is extensive, often reaching out past two to three times farther than the periphery of the tree's foliage. The part of the tree that we see above ground is the outward expression of its root system. In like manner, we cannot hide what is in our heart because the words that come out of our mouth will betray us. The Bible's scripture says it is out of the mind, out of the fullness of the heart that the mouth speaks. I believe that what we talk about, who we talk about, and the way we talk about them gives away our true self.

"Trees are the earth's endless effort to speak to the listening heavens," said the Indian born poet, novelist and Nobel laureate Rabindranath Tagore. Jane Pittman must have believed that trees could speak, or at least that they could listen, or she would not have wasted her time talking to one. There is much testimony in the sacred scripture concerning trees and how they are compared to God's children. The psalmist wrote: *And he shall be like a tree planted by the rivers of water, that bringeth forth his fruit in his season; his leaf also shall not wither; and whatsoever he doeth shall prosper* (Psalm 1:3). The Bible also calls believers in the Gospel of Jesus Christ the "trees of righteousness" (Isaiah 61:3).

A tree's growth process is analogous to the human journey. Just as what kind of nourishment it receives determines the sort of fruit it bears, what goes on in the heart and mind of man or woman will ultimately become evident in their lives.

GO DEEP

If I were a tree, I would exhort the people that I encounter to *go deep*. Do not live your life on the surface but dig farther down. There is no more compelling reminder of this than when Jesus said a tree is known by its fruit. So we, too, are known by what we say and do. A tree is not determined by its shape, size or color but by its fruit, and the fruit is determined by what you cannot see beneath the tree, just as our lives are determined by what others cannot readily see inside of us. Not by what we wear or drive, or by where we live but by what is going on in our minds.

The whole process begins in our minds. Whatever is in our thoughts is manifested in our lives. We are what we think about. We cannot have a positive reality with a negative mentality. More often than not, we are tempted to think about things that are not going to do us much good. Jesus said: *You have minds like a snake pit! How do you suppose what you say is worth anything when you are so foul-minded? It's your heart, not the dictionary, that gives meaning to your words. A good person produces good deeds and words season after season. An evil person is a blight on the orchard. Let me tell you something: Every one of these careless words is going to come back to haunt you. There will be a time of Reckoning. Words are powerful; take them seriously. Words can be your salvation. Words can also be your damnation* (Matthew 12:34-37).

"When an oak has a good root system, the winds of adversity actually strengthen rather than topple it," states author Pat J. Sikora. "In times of drought, the roots sink even deeper to find the water needed to nourish the tree. If these roots grow to the surface, the tree will die, but if they sink deep into what the world calls dirt, the tree can withstand anything. This process is hidden from the rest of the world. If the roots are strong, no one notices. If, however, they fail to take in the nourishment needed or grow deeply enough, lack becomes obvious. This growth must take place in the good seasons, before the storms hit." If you show me a strong tree, I will show you a strong root system. If you show me a tall building, I will show you a strong foundation. The taller the building above the ground the more solid the foundation has to be below ground. It is the strength and depth of the pylons upon which the building stands that determines whether the structure will be secure. It is a fact that some of us are building our lives on sinking sand but we need to build them on solid rock. The old hymn writer put it this way: "In times like these we need a savior; in times like these we need an anchor. Be sure, be very sure your anchor holds and grips the solid rock." That rock is Jesus. He is the One.

It is certain that the storms of life will come. The most frequent kinds of storms are the tempests, which flare up quickly – the ones we do not anticipate. We cannot tell when they will come, nor can we stop them from coming but the trees would say to us the answer to our worries lies in our minds. Our attempt to cope with the storms will be futile without a strong root system. Matthew 13:3-8 talks about this concept in the parable of the sower: *What do you make of this? A farmer planted seed. As he scattered the seed, some of it fell on the road, and birds ate it. Some fell in the gravel; it sprouted quickly but didn't put down roots, so when the sun came up it withered just as quickly. Some fell in the weeds; as it came up, it was strangled by the weeds. Some fell on good earth, and produced a harvest beyond his wildest dreams.*

The Book of Revelation tells us that we are the trees of righteousness proceeding out of the throne of God and the Lamb; it says there is a river just as pure as crystal and on each side of the river there is a tree that has 12 fruits (Revelation 22:1-2). Here lies the message of the trees: stand tall, go deep and don't lean. Trees do not try to do anything but be a tree. Stars do not struggle to shine, rivers do not struggle to flow, and usually trees do not struggle to grow. Should we not then be in the place where we do not have to struggle to be excellent and prosper?

THE BLESSED BONSAI

There is a little Japanese plant called the bonsai. The word bonsai means the art of growing dwarfed ornamentally-shaped trees or shrubs in small, shallow pots or trays. Although the process that created the bonsai was traditionally a mysterious brand of horticulture, it is solidified in the social, cultural and historical lifestyle of Asian people. They figured out how to maintain shape by controlling the plant's growth through selective pruning and pinching, including root pruning. The Japanese cleverly used this process to stunt great forest trees and make them into potted plants by tying up the taproot. This works because if the taproot does not go deep enough, the grower can take what was potentially a giant tree and make it into a potted plant. The concept represents what is happening to far too many of our children. Some parents are tying up their children's taproots so that their roots cannot go deep and they cannot become what they are designed to be. If this is true, those who are intended to be a great man or woman become stunted. We have developed a whole generation of potted plants, when they could have been sequoia, redwood or oak trees standing tall in the forest of faith.

There are people who evaluate others by looking at how they appear on the outside. It is hard for those same people to understand how others do so well when there seems to be no readily identifiable reason for their success. I will tell you why they do well. It is because of the way they think not because of the way they look. If our salvation depended on how we looked, none of us would make it. We need to move from the superficial to the substantial. We cannot control the weather. However, we can control our minds. Norman Vincent Peale wrote about this in his immortal classic *The Power of Positive Thinking*. "We build up the feeling of insecurity or security by how we think," Peale stated. "If in our thoughts we constantly fix attention upon sinister expectations of dire events that might happen, the result will be constantly to feel insecure."

Some parents are tying up their children's taproots so that their roots cannot go deep and they cannot become what they were designed to be. If this is true, those who were intended to be a great man or woman become stunted. We have developed a whole generation of potted plants, when they could have

**been sequoia, redwood or oak trees standing tall in
the forest of faith.**

INDIANAPOLIS: A CASE IN POINT

In the summer of 2006, I was a part of a group of ministers
that approached the mayor of Indianapolis asking him to
lead a public and private initiative to address some of the
problems that were destroying our community. We were
particularly concerned with the growing murder rate and
the lack of opportunities for youth and young adults, working families and ex-prisoners who sought help in getting
their lives back on track, when there was little assistance
available to them. We expressed concern that the government was headed in the wrong direction by pursuing a
policy to spend $1 billion on a new sports stadium and
expand convention and tourism facilities over investing
in its citizens. We signed an open letter to then Mayor Bart
Peterson, which was published by *The Indianapolis Star* on
August 16, 2006. We began the letter by commending the
mayor for his response to the rising homicides, primarily
through the city's increased law enforcement activities:

**"The measures you and other public officials have taken
are needed but long overdue," we wrote. "However,
they treat only the symptoms and not the cause of our
current chaos... What good will it do for us to have
a new stadium that we are afraid to go to for fear of**

being robbed or murdered? We understand the need to repair what is broken, but the safety issues are tied to social issues... Our kids need mentoring, tutoring and social skills. Our parents need training...

"We need recreation centers and after-school education centers. We need more anti-truancy, anti-drug, and anti-teenage-pregnancy programs. We need more early-childhood programs."

Additionally, we asked the mayor to lead an initiative to raise at least $25 million per year from public and private sources in the next 12 months, which would be used to expand and strengthen social and community organizations as well as create new opportunities through faith-based initiatives and other programs.

An editorial published in *The Indianapolis Star* on the same day concurred with our position. It stated, "If the surge in violent crime that has plagued the city, especially the black community, is to be turned back then investments must be made in people, not just in policing and prosecution. Tutoring, mentoring, job training and parent training are key in the battle against crime. Counseling for teens who are at risk of drug abuse, pregnancy and quitting school also need to be addressed. Many are the threads of the social fabric that protects families and neighborhoods, and they are unraveling. Unless they are restored, crime is inevitable and unstoppable."

The city was reluctant to embrace our proposal so in January 2007, I wrote another letter to the same newspaper about the same problem: "Go ahead and build the stadium for $1 billion, build the library for $200 million, build new hotels for mega-millions, get new police uniforms for $1 million, give police officers a well-deserved raise, give the City-County Council a raise, spend millions on a downtown sidewalk. But remember, a city is only as great as its people.

"If we can find the money for all these projects, why can't we find the money to curb crime by investing in our youth and young adults, the poor and disenfranchised? Twenty-five million dollars does not sound like much when you compare it to the spending frenzy taking place in our city. Our children and our grandchildren are being left behind. As I indicated in my book, *The Home Alone Syndrome,* we are not so much a *lost* generation as we are a *left* generation. We need to invest more in mentoring, tutoring, job placement and preparation, offender re-entry, anti-drug and drug treatment, parenting empowerment, and recreation programs both after school and on the weekends. We need to deal with the cause and not just the crisis. We treat the crisis with cops, courts, prosecutors, and prisons. The cause is poverty and ignorance. It costs far less to educate and recreate than to incarcerate."

In our discussions with the city, the group of ministers made the point that we could never be a great community if all of the attention and resources were spent on property and not people. As long as summers come and the children who need help the most have no jobs and no place to recreate, we are asking for trouble. The mayor appointed a blue ribbon commission to study these problems, which is a typical maneuver to sidestep finding real solutions. These kinds of issues do not go away they just get worse. Our city continues to live in crisis, which is not easily detectable on the surface. In other words, the tree looks good but we have a root problem. Interestingly enough, to the surprise of many the once popular Mayor Bart Peterson lost reelection in 2007. I do not know if this is a portrait of your city, but I am a firm believer that whenever a city puts property before people then we *all* lose.

'We need to invest more in mentoring, tutoring, job placement and preparation, offender re-entry, anti-drug and drug treatment, parenting empowerment, and recreation programs both after school and on the weekends. We need to deal with the cause and not just the crisis. We treat the crisis with cops, courts, prosecutors, and prisons. The cause is poverty and ignorance. It costs far less to educate and recreate than to incarcerate.'

So the question becomes where are we sowing the seeds of our future? Too many of our teenage girls are becoming pregnant and having babies outside of marriage. Not to be outdone, our boys are scattering their seeds indiscriminately and fathering children without taking responsibility for them. We are putting ourselves in a position to ruin a second generation because we do not understand that we are still called by the biblical mandate to *train up our children in the way they should go and when they are old they will not depart from it.* (Proverbs 22:6). Our parents are failing each generation by failing to understand the biblical injunction that states our *children are a heritage of the Lord: the fruit of the womb is his reward* (Psalm 127:3). Part of the problem is parents are ill-prepared to teach what they do not know. My grandmother used to say, *you cannot teach what you do not know, and you cannot lead where you will not go.*

I wrote in my book *Boys to Men*, "What we are talking about here is 'arrested development.' When our boys spend more time playing ball than time spent in the library, they are in trouble. Men are made from the inside out, not the outside in. It is a process and it is a passage, not a quick fix. But once our boys get on the journey, and feel confident the new direction is taking them where they can make something of their lives, then their hearts will be lifted." The power of the mind is evident in the outcome of our children's lives. I can guarantee you what will happen when boys stop throwing away their seed. Our families will come back into focus and our communities won't be starting off with a deficit. Our children won't be having children when they learn that their minds are ultimately in control of their libidos. Once we make up our minds that we are going to live up to biblical standards and determine that we are going to abstain from sexual activity until marriage, God will honor it. It is called right thinking. This requires a transformed mind, which comes from replacing our current mental software with the software of the Word of God.

STAND TALL

I often tell the children and their parents in our church that we are soldiers in God's army. We must learn how to stand tall. We must straighten our posture and pull up our pants! A hat on backwards or sideways can indicate the direction we are going. It does not make sense to have tattoos on our chests and nothing in our heads. What good does it do to get a weave and still be wicked? It is not what is *on* our heads but what is *in* our heads that makes the difference. There is no reason to wear a cross if we are not going to bear a cross. If we are not deep in the Word, prayer, service, giving, loving, and living, no amount of makeup can *make up* for our negligence.

If I were raising a family today, I would fight for them and for those values that are changing the minds of our children and grandchildren. I would teach them to stand tall, push their taproots deep, and spread their branches wide. By reading and studying the Bible as the Word of God, I would teach them the difference between making a living and making a difference. I would help them to see that holiness or righteousness is more important than hip-hop.

We are soldiers in God's army. We must learn how to stand tall. We must straighten our posture and pull up our pants! A hat on backwards or sideways can indicate the direction we are going. It does not make sense to have tattoos on our chests and nothing in our heads. What good does it do to get a weave and still be wicked? It is not what is *on* our heads but what is *in* our heads that makes the difference. There is no reason to wear a cross if we are not going to bear a cross. If we are not deep in the Word, prayer, service, giving, loving, and living, no amount of makeup can *make up* for our negligence.

Think about Jane Pittman talking to the tree. She regularly practiced this as a therapeutic form of stress relief and meditation. There is a formula that if followed closely by us will bring true relief and success. When we meditate on the Bible as the Word of God, it is planted in our hearts and manifested through our actions. We must learn why we were made. We were not made to be cute or clever. We were made to make a difference and be a vessel of victory carrying the Holy Spirit. That is, witnessing and testifying to the love of God that people's lives can change for the better. I wrote the song several years ago called "Blessed to be a Blessing." The chorus goes like this: "I've been blessed to be a blessing; I've been saved to do some saving; I've been loved to do some loving; and I want the world to know, what a blessing it is to be blessed." The late pop musician, Jimi Hendrix, once said: "When the power of love overcomes the love of power the world will know peace."

We are designed by The Great Architect to be somebody and make a difference. All that is required is for us to operate in the purpose that God has chosen for us. That purpose is found throughout the Bible, which is our road map in discovering our destiny. Such promises portend great things for believers who live expecting to be blessed. Once we discover our purpose, we can live an abundant life, full of joy, peace, love, happiness, long suffering and self-control. If we have the fruit of the Spirit, we are walking in love, and if we are walking in love we can change the world.

Chapter 3
The Burning Bush: Religion vs. Relationship

*'We have just enough religion to make us hate,
but not enough to make us love one another.'
– Jonathan Swift*

You can't look at it with the naked eye. It withers fruit
on the vine and leaves men and women parched and
thirsty. If you lie under it for too long, you will get burned.
But without the sun, there could be no life on earth.
With a surface temperature of about 7,000 degrees
fahrenheit, the sun has never stopped burning. Our
solar system's largest planet seems to feed off of itself.
Nuclear-powered solar energy is created deep within
its core. Every second 700 million tons of hydrogen are
converted into helium ashes and the energy it produces
is released as light and heat.

Moses must have wondered what strange phenomenon that he was looking at when he was called to go
emancipate his people – the Israelites – from Egypt
in the story of the burning bush in ancient Midian.
Could it have been a small version of the sun, or was it
the Son? *Moses was shepherding the flock of Jethro, his
father-in-law, the priest of Midian. He led the flock to the
west end of the wilderness and came to the mountain of
God, Horeb. The angel of God appeared to him in flames*

of fire blazing out of the middle of a bush. He looked. The bush was blazing away but it didn't burn up. Moses said, "What's going on here? I can't believe this! Amazing! Why doesn't the bush burn up?" God saw that he had stopped to look. God called to him from out of the bush, "Moses! Moses!" (Exodus 3:1-4). This scriptural passage gives us perspective about the condition of the church today. It is one of the most captivating and motivating scriptures found in the Bible. It speaks to the pain and promise of faith. If simply read as an Old Testament story, it is both arresting and awesome. Moses could not figure out what made the fire keep going.

Most people only see the burning bush story as an account of God's recruiting of Moses to lead the Israelites out of their oppressive and dehumanizing bondage in Egypt. Many people believe that God supernaturally and spectacularly called Moses, but they fail to see how the account relates personally to each of their lives. Often, when we look at a story such as this, we miss those things that God is really saying to us. We do not necessarily understand that when the Lord's mouth opens, something is going to happen. When God speaks, it should fan the flames of justice and mercy toward the oppressed.

RELATIONSHIP AND RELIGION

The story of the burning bush makes me think about the difference between *relationship* and *religion*. To say it more precisely, religion seems to be part of the problem. I know this may sound strange, but a religion that does not have a personal connection with the people who believe in it can be a type of bondage all by itself. Instead of trying to persuade people to be part of a religion, I have tried to get them into relationship with the Lord Jesus Christ. John 8:36 says: *If the Son therefore shall make you free, ye shall be free indeed.* If you have a *relationship* with Jesus, that is different than just having *religion.* For religion sees God as being outside, or as hovering up there somewhere, invisible, looking down upon us. In reality, the Lord occupies the space right next to us and speaks to us through an inner burning bush. In other words, in religion God is a kind of Wizard of Oz orchestrating and manipulating mankind from behind a distant curtain. In this way of thinking, people view the Lord as a cosmic bellboy, who is waiting at our beck and call to do whatever it is that we want Him to do. We ring the bell and He is supposed to come running to fulfill our desires. I like what Max Lucado said in his wonderful book *Next Door Savior,* "Our God is near enough to touch and strong enough to trust." In other words, the hip-hop interpretation is Jesus is alive in the 'hood.

God is both transcendent and imminent. Traditional religion focuses on the transcendent God while relationship focuses on the imminent God – the one inside of us. Am I talking about two Gods? No, God is omnipresent; so when I say He is up there and inside of us at the same time, I am really saying the Lord is everywhere at once. We do not balance our understanding of God very well. We have a tendency to focus on the Creator when it is convenient but do not necessarily understand God's power. We need a right thinking balance. As a man thinketh…

For religion sees God as being outside, or as hovering up there somewhere, invisible, looking down upon us. In reality, the Lord occupies the space right next to us and speaks to us through an inner burning bush. In other words, in religion God is a kind of Wizard of Oz orchestrating and manipulating mankind from behind a distant curtain. In this way of thinking, people view the Lord as a cosmic bellboy, who is waiting at our beck and call to do whatever it is that we want Him to do.

The account of the burning bush is not just a spiritual story because how we read it, hear it, and think about it has everything to do with how we live our lives in response to this incredible story. To get the results we want, we will need to move from *looking* at the bush to *being* the bush. There is a huge difference between you reading about a burning bush that fails to consume itself and actually being that bush, a burning within you. If you could ever make the bush burn in you by a leap of faith, it would dramatically change everything. Think for a moment what would happen if you would not just view it as a bush in flames on a mountainside but see the bush burning incessantly within you – one with an eternal fire. Some people would question how God could be in a bush, but if you have a relationship with the Lord, you already know that God works in mysterious ways. If you have a relationship with the Master, you also know that God can be anywhere and everywhere at the same time. After all, He is God all by Himself who made everything out of nothing! Right there He has got my vote.

To get the results we want, we will need to move from *looking* at the bush to being the bush. There is a huge difference between you reading about a burning bush that fails to consume itself and actually being that bush, a bush burning within you. If you could ever make the bush burn in you by a leap of faith, it would dramatically change everything.

A BURNING NEED TO EDUCATE

Our congregation takes time each fall to bless teachers and students as they go back to school because we know how important education is to our community and our nation. As I have said before, if people would take a hard look at the educational levels of felons and the so-called criminal element, they would see the role that learning plays in developing responsible and productive citizens and preventing them from entering and returning to the criminal justice system. The U.S. Department of Justice's Bureau of Justice Statistics reported in 2008 that 68 percent of the nearly 2 million people held in jails or prisons in the United States had not earned a high school diploma. Only 26 percent of those inmates managed to acquire a GED while serving time in a correctional facility. If recent incarceration rates remain unchanged, 1 of every 15 persons in the U.S., or 6.6 percent of the population, will serve time in prison during their lifetimes, according to the Bureau's estimates. The chance of going to prison is 18.6 percent for blacks, 10 percent for Hispanics and 3.4 percent for whites during their lifetimes. Incredibly, the Bureau predicts that "based on the current rates of first incarceration, an estimated 32 percent of Black males will enter State or Federal prison during their lifetimes, compared to 17 percent of Hispanic males and 5.9 percent of White males." I have noticed that when the media reports crime, they give every statistic except the education level of the accused. If this were to happen, you would see a powerful correlation between education, or the lack thereof, and crime. We must understand the foolishness of our stewardship when we fail to realize it takes more money to incarcerate than it does to educate. We must learn that it is wiser for us to lift them up than to just lock them up.

You can go to college and still go wrong. Conversely, you can miss college and still go right. Yet an overwhelming portion of the dysfunction in our community is related to our lack of education. The United Negro College Fund theme has it right: *A mind is a terrible thing to waste!* It is our responsibility as parents to make sure our children go to school. Our youths could move from just looking at the bush to becoming the bush if we could get this new generation of parents to make education a priority and support them in their studies. We cannot allow children to just sit at home and waste their time in front of a television set or a video game. We have to have a zero tolerance on truancy. We have got to get the iPods out of their ears and some knowledge in their heads.

We must understand the foolishness of our steward-ship when we fail to realize it takes more money to incarcerate than it does to educate. We must learn that it is wiser for us to lift them up than to just lock them up.

Teachers, no matter how dedicated they are, have a tough time fulfilling their noble mission when they are trying to lead students who will not cooperate. Especially, when we undervalue teachers and under-appreciate them. I have always been a strong advocate of raising teachers' salaries, as well as raising the expectation of teachers in the classroom. In an era where children are raising children, we need teachers who are well paid to fill in the gaps that juvenile parents have left unfulfilled. Some of the teachers – certainly not all of them – need to lead by example in terms of what they wear to school each day and how they conduct themselves in front of students. I am thankful to God that we have an unusual number of educators in our church and have always appreciated the people who value education. But I usually notice a disturbing fact about the teachers that we honor every year. That is, female educators usually outnumber their male colleagues by a ratio of at least 10 to 1. This concerns a reality that does not always speak well to our situation because of the number of boys being raised in single, mostly female-headed households in our community.

We have got to get the iPods out of their ears and some knowledge in their heads.

In my book, *The Home Alone Syndrome*, I asked the following questions: Who is going to turn the music, television and video games off when boys and girls come home from school and see to it that they do their homework? Who is going to teach them to be responsible for their actions in school, and for their grades? Who is going to teach their sons to respect protocol at activities, and to be punctual about time commitments and class schedules? Today, every urban school needs to provide parenting classes as a requirement for registration. This is particularly important in the elementary grade levels.

Nevertheless, every student, especially young black males, needs to understand the power of education and that educators have one of the most important jobs in the world. Most of our children are not going to make it to the NFL, NBA, WNBA, or become stars in pro baseball, golf or tennis, despite the dreams that some of them carry of being sports celebrities. For example, there are only about 450 athlete positions available in the NBA. This suggests there are long odds for the millions of young girls and boys who dream of becoming a Kobe Bryant, Tamika Catchings, LaDainian Tomlinson or Venus Williams. It would make better sense for parents to encourage their children to become teachers instead of paid athletes. Being a teacher is one of the most powerful careers they could ever have. I am eternally grateful for all of the teachers, counselors, principals and other administrators who seek to provide covering for our children and work extremely hard to impart wisdom and knowledge to them. I pray that they may not *grow weary in well doing, for in due season they shall reap, if they faint not* (Galatians 6:9). I am particularly thankful for each classroom teacher and hope that when they feel discouraged, they will remember there is a God who rules above with a hand of power and a heart of love, and He will fight their battles if they will just stand still and listen to the leadership of the Holy Spirit.

I appreciate so much what my friend, Indianapolis Public Schools Superintendant, Dr. Eugene G. White, did in bringing a student uniform policy to that school district in the 2007-2008 school term. Dr. White, who was born to a 17-year-old single mother in rural Alabama in 1947, proved through his own considerable achievements that a student can excel when faced with adverse circumstances while growing up. That is what I call leadership. I wrote the following in my books *Boys to Men,* and *Mama's Boy,* because I, too, was raised by a single-parent grandmother: Many of us have been raised by women who did their best, worked their hardest, sacrificed and saved for us. My grandmother was such a woman. I could not appreciate her more but as a female, she could not be to me what a father could be. A woman cannot teach a boy to be a man. It takes a man to do that. In like manner, a father cannot be to his daughter what a mother can be. It takes a woman to do that.

"Many of us have been raised by women who did their best, worked their hardest, sacrificed and saved for us. My grandmother was such a woman. I could not appreciate her more but as a female, she could not be to me what a father could be. A woman cannot teach a boy to be a man. It takes a man to do that. In like manner, a father cannot be to his daughter what a mother can be. It takes a woman to do that."

MANY ARE CALLED

God can call you out of the most unusual circumstances, just as He did Moses from the midst of a burning bush. When the Lord calls a man, He does not always do it in church. When God calls a woman, it is not in front of the sanctuary altar every single time. As a matter of fact, God can call you on the backside of the Midian Desert. He can call you out of a garbage can, off of a bar stool and straight out of a drug house. It is sad that some of us can miss His voice because we only look to hear it while we are in church or in some other orthodox way. The God that I know works in mysterious ways. For instance, you can be driving your car down some lonely road and He can stop you, speak to you, and give you orders from headquarters that it is time to live a new life. He is full of surprises. God's identity and purpose are not limited to the laws of nature. We must not try to put God in the same box that we put ourselves. God is bigger than the box. He is unlimited in His ability to express Himself, and He comes to reshape and recreate us in a new way. God is Malachi's refiners fire: *But who will be able to stand up to that coming? Who can survive His appearance? He'll be like white-hot fire from the smelter's furnace. He'll be like the strongest lye soap at the laundry. He'll take his place as a refiner of silver, as a cleanser of dirty clothes. He'll scrub the Levite priests clean, refine them like gold and silver, until they're fit for God, fit to present offerings of righteousness* (Malachi 3:2-3).

If you believe that God is in the bush and can show up anytime He wants to show up, and speak any way He wants to speak, then you can move to the next level. Then you will believe that *God is a spirit: and they that worship Him must worship Him in spirit and in truth* (John 4:24). When you have this sort of relationship with God, you will come to realize that the Lord is not a man but a

Spirit that cannot be consumed. You will know that you are the sanctuary of God and that He dwells in you. You will know that the church is just the building but you are the temple. And all this time you have been going to church thinking that was the only place you could find God. But the truth is we are the temple, the bush that God lives in. That uncontainable, un-consumable, incredible, unpredictable Spirit of God is in us! Do you understand the difference between religion and that? The most powerful spirit that can ever be is in us. The speaking spirit that packs more power than a nuclear explosion on the face of the sun is in us. If God is in the bush and He is in us, then we are the burning bush for which He has been searching. We cannot be contained, nor can we be consumed. We are God's trusted treasure. We are not trash because God does not make any junk.

We must not try to put God in the same box that we put ourselves. God is bigger than the box. He is unlimited in His ability to express Himself, and He comes to reshape and recreate us in a new way.

"God never shows up in something that looks the way you think it should look," wrote E. Bernard Jordan in *The Laws of Thinking*. "He always buries the treasure in a vessel that looks unlike it would hold the treasure." As I have said before from the pulpit, the scripture teaches in

2 Corinthians 4:7-11 that *we have this treasure in earthen vessels, that the excellency of the power may be of God, and not of us. We are troubled on every side, yet not distressed; we are perplexed, but not in despair; Persecuted, but not forsaken; cast down, but not destroyed; Always bearing about in the body the dying of the Lord Jesus, that the life also of Jesus might be made manifest in our body. For we which live are always delivered unto death for Jesus' sake, that the life also of Jesus might be made manifest in our mortal flesh.*

Isaiah 53:5 said, *He was bruised for our iniquities* and *with His stripes we are healed.* We are walking around with the body of Christ in us, with His bruises in us and on us, knowing that if the Spirit that was also in Him is in us, it will quicken our mortal bodies, raise us from the dead, and make us brand new in Jesus.

And all this time you have been going to church thinking that was the only place you could find God. But the truth is we are the temple, the bush that God lives in. That uncontainable, un-consumable, incredible, unpredictable spirit of God is in us! Do you understand the difference between religion and that? The most powerful spirit that can ever be is in us. The speaking spirit that packs more power than a nuclear explosion on the face of the sun is in us. If God is in the bush and He is in us, then we are

the burning bush that He has been looking for. We cannot be contained, nor can we be consumed. We are God's trusted treasure. We are not trash because God does not make any junk.

It is time for us to realize that Christianity is not about a religion but it is about a relationship with God in Christ.

Since He is a burning bush, guess what He is in you? That makes you a burning bush, too. Therefore, neither He nor you can be consumed or contained. For this reason, I implore you to stop looking at the bush and start being that bush. It is time to quit *staring* from a distance at a fire that burns without ceasing and start *being* that fire.

Every flame is a light. You can express the unquenchable burning bush in you by letting *your light so shine before men, that they might see your good works, and glorify your Father which is in heaven* (Matthew 5:16). Jesus encourages us take the basket off of the light because we are the light of the world. *Ye are the salt of the earth: but if the salt have lost his savour, wherewith shall it be salted? It is thenceforth good for nothing, but to be cast out, and to be trodden under foot of men. Ye are the light of the world. A city that is set on an hill cannot be hid* (Matthew 5:13-14).

You might say, "Oh, I am not worthy." The truth of the matter is that none of us are worthy. But we become worthy by the blood of Jesus. If we would just get in touch with who we really are, we could serve God with a new level of dedication and a new fervor of enthusiasm because we would finally recognize that we are not just looking at that burning bush, we are that burning bush. There is no way I can be casual or cavalier or complacent now that I really know who God is in me. I can serve Him with a new level of dedication because I am a burning bush on fire for God.

As I have often said from the pulpit, once you catch on fire people will come from near and far to see you burn. It is the key to the law of attraction. The Apostle Paul said, *Christ in you, the hope of glory* (Colossians 1:27). The key to getting the burning bush in you is listening for the Lord's voice. Do not wait until you go to church. Open up your Bible. Open up your heart and mind and let Him come in now. He is trying to speak to you – trying to tell you something. He said: *Behold, I stand at the door, and knock: if any man hear my voice, and open the door, I will come in to him, and will sup with him, and he with Me* (Revelation 3:20).

You are somebody very special. Once you embrace this, I believe this means that you are a burning bush, you are God's treasure in a chest, and you are a child of God. Once you realize that you are the temple of the Holy Spirit or the burning bush, you cannot be consumed nor defeated. It is all about relationship *with* Jesus and not religion *about* Jesus. Once again, there is a difference between religion and relationship, and that difference makes *all* of the difference in the world. What do you think? Remember, it's all in your mind.

Chapter 4
Think Love!

'When the power of love overcomes the love of power, the world will know peace.' – Jimi Hendrix

I have some friends in Atlanta named Edgar and Ida. At age 23, Edgar was diagnosed with polycystic kidney disease, a hereditary kidney ailment involving more than one kidney. He checked himself into a hospital to learn more about his condition. Edgar had two questions for the attending physician. He wanted to know how long his kidneys would last, and how long he had to live. He was told his kidneys would hold out for about 20 years, after which he would need a transplant in order to survive.

Just as the doctor had predicted, when Edgar reached age 43, the mass of cysts on each of his kidneys began to burst, which would eventually damage the organs' filtering process. If the condition was left untreated, poisonous toxins would kill him. Edgar began dialysis in July 1990 at age 43. He dialyzed three days per week for 18 years, trekking around the country, never stopping his work career. His stamina and resilience were remarkable, to say the least. He was in and out of the hospital and at times seemed to face imminent death. But whenever things looked the bleakest, Edgar awoke from unconsciousness with the biggest smile you ever saw. This always caused the nurses to remark, "This man is made of steel." Edgar would just grin and retort, "No, this man is made from God." The nurses would just shed tears. Edgar received a kidney transplant on February 4, 2007, due to the unfortunate and untimely death of a 21-year-old man who died in an automobile accident. Edgar was in the hospital for only five days for the operation – including one day in very critical condition. Remarkably, he was back at work in just four months. He returned to his job completely healthy and smiling every single day.

How did he endure the trauma of a life-threatening illness? Edgar had a positive attitude, was a strong disciplinarian and enjoyed lots of loving family support. In addition, he has never lived his life thinking what he could not do. On the contrary, he lived it and continues to live life thinking what he *can* do. Nearly every time Edgar woke up in the hospital, the first thing he would ask is "Where's my wife and where are my glasses," in that order.

Edgar will always be grateful to the young man whose death allowed his life on earth to continue. To give someone else one of your organs is a supreme example of unconditional love. This is reinforced in the scripture where it says: *This is my command: Love one another the way I loved you. This is the very best way to love. Put your life on the line for your friends* (John 15:12-13).

There are too many folks who put their hopes in religion but forget to love. Someone can have plenty of religion and still be thinking wrong. Although Islam is well respected as a world religion, Islamic extremists give this religion a bad name. They claim to have religion, but there is something going on in their interpretation of that religion that produces wrong thinking. As a result, what we see again and again is chaos and conflict emanate from what the Islamic extremists call religion. Wars fueled by religious extremism and hatred in Iraq and Afghanistan have taken the lives of tens of thousands of people. The Iraq war in and of itself is an example of wrong thinking and its inception was based on lies, deception and revenge. This in essence constitutes the antithesis of love. We also see this phenomenon even among Christian fanatics, such as so called Christian militia groups and the Ku Klux Klan. They would all argue that they are very religious, but their thinking is perverted in that they call for death and destruction rather than life and love.

Anytime there are people who claim they want to preserve life, yet the same people take life with terrorist actions, tells us immediately that no matter how much education they have, it is wrong thinking. Because what we think about is what we bring about, it is crucial to have our minds on the right thing. Paul, the great New Testament writer, said, *Summing it all up, friends, I'd say you'll do best by filling your minds and meditating on things true, noble, reputable, authentic, compelling, gracious – the best, not the worst; the beautiful, not the ugly; things to praise, not things to curse. Put into practice what you learned from me, what you heard and saw and realized. Do that, and God, who makes everything work together, will work you into His most excellent harmonies.* (Philippians 4:8-9).

Another example in our nation is what is happening in regard to the killing of the innocent. What kind of thinking allows us to cannibalize our own children? There is example after example where parents and adults have murdered or maimed their children. The national phenomenon of killing our children is a powerful example of contemporary wrong thinking. In just the first six weeks of 2008, four pre-teen children were homicide victims in Indianapolis compared to five there in all of 2007. Those cases were heartbreaking. In January 2008, a 23-month-old child and a 5-month-old child were shot to death along with their mothers in an apparent botched robbery attempt infamously named the Indianapolis Hovey Street murders. The Hovey street murders were one of the most startling cases ever seen. Armed thugs, looking for drugs, broke into a home killing two babies in the arms of their mothers. Four people died that night because of wrong thinking. It is just one of many examples where people have literally lost their minds. Before the month was out, a 28-year-old man shot his 8-year-old daughter to death, before taking his own life, after arguing with the child's mother. Nine days later, an 8-year-old, second grade girl was struck and killed by a bullet, fired from outside the house, as she sat watching television. Then, shockingly in February, a 2-year-old boy was smothered to death in Indianapolis after his drunken mother passed out on top of him.

TWAHCD

Many of the problems that we are dealing with today have been brought about by our own actions, despite the fact that we have had a tendency to blame others for those predicaments. We do not like to take the blame for our own actions. Instead, we sometimes justify the problems that we have created by making the devil the fall guy. Our reasoning goes, "The devil did it," or "The devil made me do it." But the simple fact is that so much of the challenges, chaos, and confusion in our lives is created by our own disobedience. These difficulties are usually a product of our minds and the way we think. If we think unlovely thoughts, especially unlovely thoughts about other people, unloveliness will be produced in our lives.

James Allen wrote, "Let a man radically alter his thoughts, and he will be astonished at the rapid transformation it will effect in the material conditions of his life. Men imagine that thought can be kept secret, but it cannot. It rapidly crystallizes into habit, and habit solidifies into circumstance."

I have heard it said: "Watch your thoughts, they become your words. Watch your words, they become your actions. Watch your actions, they become your habits.

Watch your habits, they become your character. Watch your character, it becomes your destiny." I have coined the acronym for this TWAHCD (pronounced tee-wah-cee-dee). It stands for thoughts, words, actions, habits, character and destiny.

One way we can begin to tell whether or not we are a loving person, and whether people love us has to do with how much love we are putting out, if any. If we sow love, we get love. It is called *The law of the harvest,* or put another way *The law of attraction*. Here is how it goes: What we put out, we get back. What we give out, we attract. The law of the harvest and the law of attraction are the same as the law of love because the law of love is what creates and helps make everything else possible. Conversely, when we create an atmosphere of suspicion and mistrust that is what we will receive in return.

'Watch your thoughts, they become your words. Watch your words, they become your actions. Watch your actions, they become your habits. Watch your habits, they become your character. Watch your character, it becomes your destiny.

STRONG TOWER OF LOVE

Rhonda Byrne wrote in *The Secret*, "When you want to attract something into your life, make sure your actions don't contradict your desires." If we walk around with our guard up all the time, always acting defensive, or with a chip on our shoulders, then we should not expect to be treated any differently by others. If we are always dealing with a fair amount of chaos in our lives, the probability is high that our thought patterns are contributing to the confusion. If we can drop those things and begin to think love, forgiveness and mercy, that is what we will get back.

During my entire life, people have loved me in spite of my faults. That is why I can love others in spite of theirs. In more than 40 years of ministry, I have discovered that people can attend church, have the *look* about them, wear the outfit, but if they leave church and return home to create an atmosphere of constant confusion, obviously, the way that they look in church does not tell the whole story. The writer of 1 John, who was probably the Apostle John, broke it down this way: *My beloved friends, let us continue to love each other since love comes from God. Everyone who loves is born of God and experiences a relationship with God. The person who refuses to love doesn't know the first thing about God, because God is love – so you can't know Him if you don't love.* (1 John 4:7-8).

Even after you have made up your mind that you are going to show love, it will not be easy to do. You have to *think love first* before you can express love through your actions. I can easily tell whether or not people are born of God. If they show love, trust and unconventional acceptance, then those people are clearly operating in God. It does not matter what denomination they belong to or what church they attend. Everyone, who is born of God, is born of love. If we are evil, mean-spirited and religious on Sunday but a hellion on Monday through Friday then we are not operating in love.

What I pray for regularly is that God would make me a strong tower of love. I want to be perceived as a person who can love unconditionally. I want to guard against just loving people because of who they are or what status they have attained in life. That is not the way I want to be seen. Instead I want to love them, if for no other reason than because God loves them. When we express love, we are actually expressing the power of God. Unfortunately, the truth is there are times when people claim to have God's love, but they won't even speak to the person sitting next to them at church. Some of them rationalize their bad manners by saying to themselves: "Well, I spoke to her and she did not speak back." This sort of inconsiderate reasoning has nothing to do with love. People who mistreat us may not have grown to the same spiritual level that we have attained yet. As a matter of fact, the very love that we show them, in spite of their negative treatment toward us, is the main experience that will help them grow as Christians. When we show them love, they cannot help but to say to themselves, "Well, that is a nice person. What is wrong with me that

I do not speak?" Again, we reap just what we sow. This always reminds me of the story about the little boy who went to the mountain top and hollered these words across the valley, "I hate you. I hate you. I hate you." And the words came back to him in a forceful echo: "I hate you. I hate you. I hate you." It frightened him so much that he ran home and told his father that someone on the other side of the valley hates you. His father told him to go back to the same place and say, "I love you. I love you. I love you." The little boy did exactly that and discovered a voice that said, "I love you. I love you. I love you." That mountain top experience changed his life forever. Have you been to the mountain top?

Without a doubt, it is not easy to love those who are unlovely. There are some people who just won't let us love them – not for all of the tea in China. Some people, no matter what we say to them, still will not speak because they are just plain mean-spirited. These are often the sort of people who claim to be *religious*. They will argue you down declaring what church they belong to, how long they have been going there, what their denomination is, and how they are filled with the "Holy Ghost." There is only one problem with their fussing: The Bible says if you are of God, you must be of love. *And now abide faith, hope, love, these three; but the greatest of these is love.* (1 Corinthians 13:13). When you tell people that they could stand to show a little more love, you get this kind of response: "Now hold on, I am a person of faith." That is all well and good, but even faith works by love (Galatians 5:6). Be wary of folks who claim to have so much *faith*, yet they do not have any love. They can quote scripture and claim they can walk on water but show very little love. The scripture admonishes us to be careful about such people.

We have a bunch of people all over the body of Christ who are great Bible people in the sense that they have a Bible and highlighters – in different colors – along with three notebooks, yet they have not loved anybody. They may even have three or four Bibles of different sizes but show no love. They are so busy taking notes that they do not even speak. There is nothing in the world wrong with taking notes, but remember that love is about relationship toward one another and not membership in a church. We can easily miss the blessing that God has prepared to give us, through the person sitting next to us, if we shun that person. We can be so busy being a student and taking notes that we fail to share with them our humility and love. This same thought was expressed in my book *The Home Alone Syndrome*, when I wrote: "The power is turned on when you realize only the truly great are humble – and only the humble are truly great."

Even faith works by love. Be wary of folks who claim to have so much faith, yet they do not have any love. They can quote scripture and claim they can walk on water but show very little love. The

scripture admonishes us to be careful about such people.

═══════════════════════════════════════

My friend, the late Norman Vincent Peale, relayed that there is one basic character trait, which is critical in helping people to like us. "That trait is sincere and forthright interest in and love for people," he wrote in *The Power of Positive Thinking*. "Perhaps if you cultivate this basic trait, other traits will naturally develop." This sort of truth can especially guide us in relationships. I have often found favor with people because I have sought to love them and engage them even though I did not know them. I have received great rewards when I risk coming out of myself and embracing the stranger. It happens with store clerks, on the street, and everywhere I go. I have often thought that we miss a blessing when we fail to express the best of our humanity. In other words, human beings were made *with* love and *to* love one another. It begins with a thought. It is expressed often by just speaking to or smiling at another person. This is how love begins. It is not as deep as it is deliberate. It is not as mystical as it is a ministry of thinking love every day in every way.

A HOUSE DIVIDED

We are living in a time and culture when division has almost become the norm. The red states against the blue states; White folks against Black folks; yellow against brown; rich against poor; Sunni against Shiite, and Islam against Christianity. You name it and we have found a way to divide it. We find ourselves congregating in public and private with people who look just like us. Our immaturity shows itself when we restrict our social interaction only to people we feel comfortable with and embrace the narrow-mindedness of group thinking. Our childishness is evident when we can only relate to people in our racial, social-economic or ethnic group. Our honesty comes into doubt when we only love the *special people* of our society. This type of wrong-headed thinking prohibits the manifestation and generosity of who God truly wants to be to us. So many of us are living below our privileges, far beneath what God has intended for us that we are actually shortchanging ourselves. We can not think negatively about ourselves or others and expect to get positive results. If we want a great life, we must not just love our friends. Instead, we must stretch our faith and love toward people that do not look like us, act like us, and do not even like us. We have simply got to learn how to love our enemies. What a revolutionary idea from a revolutionary named Jesus of Nazareth.

The type of wrong thinking I am talking about here is based on a flawed foundation. It bases its ideas on hearsay – he says, she says, and they say. On the other hand, right thinking has a foundation of faith. It is based on what God says through the Holy Spirit. This is a great example of the difference between prophetic and pathetic living. To live prophetically, we have to live by the Bible as the Word of God. To put it simply, God said it, I believe it, and that settles it. When I act upon it, it becomes my reality.

We cannot think negatively about ourselves or others and expect to get positive results. If we want a great life, we must not just love our friends. Instead, we must stretch our faith and love toward people that do not look like us, act like us, and do not even like us. We have simply got to learn how to love our enemies. What a revolutionary idea from a revolutionary named Jesus of Nazareth.

THE FLESH

The root of our problems could not be any clearer – it is our flesh or ego. When the flesh rises up, it stops us from loving our enemy. Our ego steps in and we start thinking more of ourselves than we do of other people. We begin making ourselves out to be better than them. In fact the word EGO stands for *"edging God out."* In order to subdue the flesh, we will have to renew the mind. Paul encourages believers to do so this way: *So here's what I want you to do, God helping you: Take your everyday, ordinary life – your sleeping, eating, going-to-work, and walking-around life – and place it before God as an offering. Embracing what God does for you is the best thing you can do for Him. Don't become so well-adjusted to your culture that you fit into it without even thinking.*

Instead, fix your attention on God. You'll be changed from the inside out. Readily recognize what He wants from you, and quickly respond to it. Unlike the culture around you, always dragging you down to its level of immaturity, God brings the best out of you, develops well-formed maturity in you (Romans 12:1-2). We must be not conformed to this world but be transformed by going to church, reading a Bible and regenerating our minds through the Word of God. There is no use in having a Bible if we are not going to use it. It is a waste of time going to church and hearing a message if we are not going to act upon what we heard! I made the point in *The Home Alone Syndrome,* "Our churches are too inflexible and insecure. Holiness is a life-style, not a dress style. We can be so heavenly minded that we are no earthly good."

Some of us are so bound up in unforgiveness that we cannot get any further in life because the grudges we are holding prevent us from a breakthrough. To put it another way, as long as we have our foot on somebody else's neck, it is true that they cannot get up. But by the same token we can't move either. *And when you assume the posture of prayer, remember that it's not all asking. If you have anything against someone, forgive – only then will your heavenly Father be inclined to also wipe your slate clean of sins* (Mark 11:25).

As long as we have our foot on somebody else's neck, it is true that they cannot get up. But by the same token we can't move either.

Unforgiveness is the most effective device that Satan uses to prevent the flow of God's blessings from reaching us. *At that point Peter got up the nerve to ask, 'Master, how many times do I forgive a brother or sister who hurts me? Seven?' Jesus replied, 'Seven! Hardly. Try seventy times seven'* (Matthew 18:21-22). Unforgiveness is wrong thinking. It makes you think you are holding someone else down but in actuality, you are holding yourself down.

THE GREATEST

Paul wrote that love is the greatest force of all: *And regardless of what else you put on, wear love. It's your basic, all-purpose garment. Never be without it* (Colossians 3:14). What is love? Someone else has described it this way: "It is silence when our words would hurt. It is patience when our neighbor is curt. It is deafness when a scandal flows. It is thoughtfulness for others' woes. It is promptness when stern duty calls and courage when misfortune falls. Love's prerogative is that love ever gives, forgives, outlives and stands with open hands. While it lives, it gives for this is love's prerogative to give and give and give." On top of that, the biblical scripture is very clear about how much love people are to give others: *You're familiar with the old written law, 'Love your friend' and its unwritten companion, 'Hate your enemy.' I'm challenging that. I'm telling you to love your enemies. Let them bring out the best in you, not the worst. When someone gives you a hard time, respond with the energies of prayer, for then you are working out of your true selves, your God-created selves.* (Matthew 5:43-44). While I know that loving your enemy can be difficult to do, this is a critical requirement to achieving an abundant life.

'It is silence when our words would hurt. It is patience when our neighbor is curt. It is deafness when a scandal flows. It is thoughtfulness for others' woes. It is promptness when stern duty calls and courage when misfortune falls. Love's prerogative is that love ever gives, forgives, outlives and stands with open hands. While it lives, it gives for this is love's prerogative to give and give and give.'

Our society must find a way to redefine love. If we were left with only five minutes in this life to talk to other people, telephone lines would be jammed with people saying, "I love you." over and over again. They would be calling people they should have said this to a long time before then but did not, and people that they wanted to say it to but let it slide. Why wait until the last five minutes? Why not say it today, in fact, why not right now? Jesus did not wait for the last five minutes. More than 2,000 years ago, He expressed His love for us through His life and sacrifice on Calvary. Because He loves us, we can love one another and because He died for us, we can live for one another. Evangelist Billy Graham said *it is later than you think and it is even later than that.*

Chapter 5
Speaking Spirits

'There is something in every one of you that waits and listens for the sound of genuine in yourself. It is the only true guide you will ever have. And if you cannot hear it, you will all of your life spend your days on the ends of strings that somebody else pulls.' – Howard Thurman

Gideon Welles was stunned at what he heard during a carriage ride in Washington, D.C., on July 13, 1862. President Abraham Lincoln had told Welles and two others, as they rode in his carriage, of his plans to end slavery through the issuance of a wartime executive proclamation.

"He dwelt earnestly on the gravity, importance, and delicacy of… emancipating the slaves by proclamation," wrote Welles in his diary, adding that Lincoln's bombshell was "A new departure for the President, for until this time… he had been prompt and emphatic in denouncing any interference by the General Government with the subject." Eight days later, Lincoln fulfilled his intentions when he read the first draft of the Emancipation Proclamation to his Cabinet. The document stated in part: "I, as Commander-in-Chief of the Army and Navy of the United States do order and declare that on the first day of January in the year of Our Lord one thousand, eight hundred and sixty three, all persons held as slaves within any state or states, wherein the constitutional authority of the United States shall not then be practically recognized, submitted to, and maintained, shall then, thenceforward, and forever, be free." Whether Lincoln knew it or not at the time, he was a speaking spirit.

Some 93 years later, a humble tailor's assistant in Montgomery, Alabama, was ordered to give up her seat on a bus. By responding curtly, "No," Rosa Lee McCauley Parks, her neck and shoulder stiff from a full day of work at the Montgomery Fair department store, was letting her spirit speak. Having just sought to buy a heating pad for her aching shoulder, at the drug store across the street from her bus stop, and tired of being pushed around, Parks' one-word declaration of 'no' revolutionized a nation. When Lincoln spoke a people were set free. When Rosa Parks spoke, a country began the long road to changing the way it treated the least of its citizens. When Dr. Martin Luther King Jr. spoke from the Lincoln Memorial those immortal words, "I have a dream," it spelled hope for a nation in crisis. Dr. King was a speaking spirit. When God spoke light was called day, and dark was called night. The Lord spoke again and the landscape was brought into formation in the midst of the waters, which separated the seas from the seas. The truth is every time God uttered words, something was created. God was the original speaking spirit. A speaking spirit is any person who allows the Holy Spirit of God to speak through him or her. The key to this concept is that it is our mouth that may be moving, but it is our spirit that is speaking. Some people just talk but others allow the spirit to speak through them. There is a difference and that difference can make all the difference in the world.

When Lincoln spoke a people were set free. When Rosa Parks spoke, a country began the long road to changing the way it treated the least of its citizens… When God spoke light was called day and dark was called night… God was the original speaking spirit.

The book of Genesis tells us that God spoke our very universe into existence: *In the beginning God created the heaven and the earth. And the earth was without form, and void; and darkness was upon the face of the deep. And the spirit of God moved upon the face of the waters. And God said, Let there be light: and there was light* (Genesis 1:1-3). Pay close attention to the phrase "and God said." God repeated that phrase 9 times in the first chapter of Genesis. This is powerful proof that the God of creation has given us a pattern to pull down strongholds and believe things that are not as though they were by thinking and then speaking things into existence.

MADE IN HIS IMAGE

Next, God created man and woman from dust. They were made into the highest form of His creation. Eugene H.

Peterson's translation of the Bible says that we are made godlike creatures. God made mankind to be godlike and reflect His image on purpose. His intention was for us to have dominion over everything else that He formed. On top of that, God made sure that there was full provision to meet every imaginable need we have.

God spoke: "Let us make human beings in our image, make them reflecting our nature so they can be responsible for the fish in the sea, the birds in the air, the cattle, and, yes, earth itself, and every animal that moves on the face of earth. God created human beings; He created them godlike, reflecting God's nature. He created them male and female. God blessed them: 'Prosper! Reproduce! Fill the earth! Take charge! Be responsible for fish in the sea and birds in the air, for every living thing that moves on the face of earth (Genesis 1:26-28).

In case you did not know it, just as when God speaks things happen, you, too, are a speaking spirit. A powerful illustration of what a speaking spirit can do is the example of Jesus saying to that *mountain, Be thou removed, and be thou cast into the sea; it shall be done* (Matthew 21:21). Over and over again, Jesus encouraged us to speak the word, which ignites the faith that moves the hand of God. When Jesus said that we could move mountains, He began this important passage by using the phrase, "Say to this mountain." Pay close attention to this scripture because it is a key to faith. Jesus says *if you have faith as* *a mustard seed, you will <u>say to this mountain</u>...* Do not miss the power of those four words. If you think right, speak right and act right, you are giving God your best. The next step is to simply trust God to do the rest. That is how faith works. What mountain are you dealing with today? Is it a mountain of debt? Perhaps it is a mountain of unforgiveness? Could it be a mountain of illness? You have the power in you to address your mountains because you are made in His image and as Eugene Peterson interpreted the scripture correctly, you are godlike. If we think right, believe right, and speak right, we can say to the mountains in our lives, "Be gone with you," and those obstacles will have to go. Your tongue holds the power of life and death (Proverbs 18:21), therefore what you say is extremely important, whether it is positive or negative. You will never say what you are supposed to say until you begin to think positively with the mind of Christ. You will never think right until the mind that is in Christ is also in you (Philippians 2:5). To acquire the mind of Christ, the first thing you need is a *mind shampoo*. It is one thing to get your body baptized but another thing to get your mind, heart, and spirit baptized. When you do, you will see that the formula God used for creation is the same one you can use to improve your life.

God has created ability in us, and it is only when we get quiet, listen to His voice in us and hear Him speak through us that we begin to flow in His power. If you are baptized with the Holy Spirit, then you are compelled to flow in Holy Spirit power. I have often said when you discover your *purpose* in life you will discover your *power*. There are many folks who want the power of God but do not understand the purpose of God. Every person has to discover the *why* of his or her existence. Once you understand why you were created, then you will understand *what* you are supposed to do while you are here. I have said to people who get confused over the fact that they do not speak in tongues, which usually occurs after they have talked about this subject with our Pentecostal friends: "Here is what you need to understand, *'God is a spirit, and they that worship Him must worship Him in spirit and in truth'*" (John 4:24). I also tell them the way to know for sure that you have been baptized with the Holy Spirit is that you think, speak and act in love. The greatest evidence of the baptism of the Holy Spirit is that a believer walks in the fruit of the spirit, which is according to the biblical scripture in Galatians 5:22-23. There is no greater sign than this. Speaking in tongues has its place in scripture and in some religious traditions, but it is not the ultimate evidence of Holy Spirit baptism. The fruit of the spirit is the true evidence. The Apostle Paul strictly admonished believers to avoid using the signs of the spirit without the substance of the spirit. Paul said in 1 Corinthians 13:1: *If I speak with human eloquence and angelic ecstasy but don't love, I'm nothing but the creaking of a rusty gate.* The whole chapter of 1 Corinthians 13 is full of instruction on the key to living the Christian life.

The main point is it is not about you, it is about Him. More precisely, it is about the image of God in you. *Christ in you is the hope of glory* (Colossians 1:27). Do not let this blow your mind, but the Bible teaches us the purpose of human existence is to express the Spirit of God in a materialistic world. In other words, the purpose of our existence is to express His Spirit in a broken, sinful, and selfish world. When we are at our best, we are spirits speaking and moving in Him. By the same token, when we are outside of the Holy Spirit of God, we find ourselves living below our privileges. Under such circumstances, we constitute a candle without a flame and a ship without a sail. We need the Holy Spirit to express Himself in us so that we may operate in our purpose.

Wrong thinking embraces the idea that it is all about us. Right thinking realizes that it is all about God in us. We have got to understand that nothing shall be impossible to us when God speaks through us. Some of us have been going to church for years and cannot walk in victory because we do not take the time to hear God's Spirit in us. By that, I mean we do not take time to cultivate His Spirit in us. Have you ever heard of the acronym WWJD? (What Would Jesus Do?) The fact of the matter is that when we speak out of the Spirit, we do what Jesus would do. How else do you think so bold, brash, and audacious a statement could be made such as "Nothing shall be impossible to you?" You may have been saying all these years, "Yes, I want to believe a statement like that, but how could this be?" The truth is it cannot be believed in the flesh but if the Spirit of God speaks through you, everything that He said He will do, God *will* do!

"The words we speak have a direct and definite effect upon our thoughts," wrote Norman Vincent Peale in the immortal classic *The Power of Positive Thinking*. "Thoughts create words, for words are the vehicles of ideas. But words also affect thoughts and help to condition if not to create attitudes. In fact, what often passes for thinking starts with talk."

The main point is it is not about you, it is about Him. More precisely, it is about the image of God in you. *Christ in you is the hope of glory* (Colossians 1:27). Do not let this blow your mind, but the Bible teaches us the purpose of human existence is to express the Spirit of God in a materialistic world. In other words, the purpose of our existence is to express His Spirit in a broken, sinful, and selfish world. When we are at our best, we are spirits speaking and moving in Him. By the same token, when we are outside of the Holy Spirit of God we find ourselves living below our privileges. Under such circumstances, we constitute a candle without a flame and a ship without a sail. We need the Holy Spirit to express Himself in us so that we may operate in our purpose.

When we learn we are not just flesh and blood but a house sheltering and clothing the Spirit of the Lord made in His very image, we discover that our authority, walk and talk changes because we are then truly representing Him. When we get to know the Word of God, we can speak the Word and it will unleash the same power that God releases when He speaks. You and I are not just flesh and blood, but our eternal life is connected to the fact that we are speaking spirits, believing in and receiving things that we never thought were possible before. We have put far, far too much attention on what happens to us in the flesh without understanding that the important part is what happens to us in the spirit world. With this knowledge, we will realize that we are bigger than our debts, circumstances, and certainly bigger than this frail frame called the body. I believe that the emptiness of our present era is because the focus has been put so intensely upon the flesh not the spirit, and people are walking around like unlit candles. There is a difference between seeing ourselves as bodies, with a spirit, rather than spirits with a body. We are a spiritual house for a body and not a physical house for a spirit.

There is a reason that we, as a people, seem to be going from pillar to post, just getting by, living below our privileges and not realizing who we are. It is because we do not know the difference between walking into a car dealer and saying, "I want a car" in the flesh, and marching in there and saying the exact same thing in the spirit. The same principle applies for strolling into a mortgage company and speaking out of flesh, versus going in there and putting everybody and everything on notice that we are in God and He is in us. When you know that you are a speaking spirit, it will make everything that you desire work in your favor. The main reason that we cannot be destroyed is because the Spirit of God is indestructible.

I believe that the emptiness of our present era is because the focus has been put so intensely upon the flesh not the spirit, and people are walking around like unlit candles. There is a difference between seeing ourselves as bodies, with a spirit, rather than spirits with a body. We are a spiritual house for a body and not a physical house for a spirit.

What keeps many people from operating through the Holy Spirit is their focus is solely on the house that their spirit lives in. I am now in my sixth decade of life, thanks be to God. The house my spirit lives in is getting old, there is a leak in the roof and water in the basement but guess what is not old? The Spirit of God in me is as young as the day the Spirit first entered me. That is why age is not the most important factor in life. I like what Leroy R. "Satchel" Paige, one of the greatest baseball players who ever lived, said: "Age is mind over matter. If you don't mind, it don't matter." That is also why the circumstances outside of us should never control us. From the very beginning, God gave us dominion over the earth and said we should never surrender it: *God spoke: Let us make human beings in our image, make them reflecting our nature. So they can be responsible for the fish in the sea, the birds in the air, the cattle, And, yes, earth itself, and every animal that moves on the face of earth* (Genesis 1:26).

Here is an example of how the Spirit works in us. Suppose you were at a point where you were looking for a mate? You should not just go around searching in the flesh and blood. I have seen too many mistakes made in the flesh. Instead it would be best to allow the Spirit of God to speak to that person that you are considering as a partner. That is, let the Holy Spirit talk to that person's spirit about your intentions. But this would not work unless you first understood who you are. So many people connect with another person based on physicality because of how they basically define themselves. They send for pictures over the Internet. We should not choose to spend our lives with people who simply look a certain way because looks change. I often tell my congregation, what was once a figure "8" could become a figure "0." So if you fell in love with an 8, what is going to happen when it becomes a 0? If you fall in love with someone who owns a lot of property and then they lose that property, where will your love go? I often tell the females in my congregation that they should not look for a Denzel in a brother, but they should look for the *divine* in that brother, and vice versa. Millions of people find themselves married and miserable because they based their choices on flesh rather than spirit. But if the Spirit of God ever became their measuring stick, these couples would really have something special.

We should not choose to spend our lives with people who simply look a certain way because looks change. I often tell my congregation, what was once a figure "8" could become a figure "0." So if you fell in love with an 8, what happens when it becomes a 0? If you fall in love with someone who owns a lot of property and then they lose that property, where will your love go? I often tell the females in my congregation that they shouldn't look for a Denzel in a brother, but they should look for the *divine* in that brother, and vice versa.

PURPOSING TO MANIFEST

The earth was without manifestation but the Spirit of God moved, and out of creation came manifestation. You see, the whole aim of creation, indeed the whole purpose of it was manifestation. God creates, but He needs a vehicle, a vessel through which He can express His Spirit.

We are hearing more and more talk about preserving and saving the earth. The environment is changing so fast that there needs to be continued discussions occurring on what is happening to our planet. For example, a National Aeronautics and Space Administration scientist disclosed in early 2008 that the earth's environment was changing faster than scientists had anticipated. "Climatic changes appear to be destabilizing vast ice sheets of western Antarctica that had previously seemed relatively protected from global warming… raising the prospect of faster sea-level rise than current estimates," *The Washington Post* reported in January 2008. Eric Rignot, a senior scientist with NASA's Jet Propulsion Laboratory, told *The Post,* "The Antarctic ice sheet is shrinking despite land temperatures for the continent remaining essentially unchanged, except for the fast-warming peninsula. Something must be changing the ocean to trigger such changes. We believe it is related to global climate forcing."

The people you hear talking about preserving and saving the earth are not irrational. If we accept God as our Father and the earth as our mother, then let's be sure to take care of our mother! After all, the Lord instructed us to be fruitful, multiply, and replenish the earth. The truth is He created man to manifest His Spirit, with each person working through the gifts that he or she has been given to express the glory of God in the world. If we really understood this, it would change the way we think. Yes, we are important to God but believe me, He can function without us. We are essential to Him because we are the vessels through which he sends His glory and expresses Himself. He absolutely wants to use us, but the Lord also said if man were to resist being used, He would use something else. Jesus once told His religious detractors that if the people didn't praise Him, the rocks would praise Him. (Luke 19:40). It is not that God cannot be God without us, it is that we cannot be what He intended us to be without Him – without His Spirit. We won't be able to worship or witness in the spirit until we understand, in essence, who we really are.

Once we have realized that He has chosen us for a special purpose, we won't allow any rocks to get in line ahead of us. God has the creative ability to use something or someone else to manifest Himself in us, but He would rather use us. The term *"ex primo"* means spirit expressed or pressed out. When we think love, we think God. By the same principle, when we speak love we express God. In the same vein, when we show love, we manifest God. If we thought the way God intended for us to think, then we would become what we thought.

Yes, we are important to God but believe me, He can function without us. We are essential to Him because we are the vessels through which he sends His glory and expresses Himself. He absolutely wants to use us, but the Lord also said if man were to resist being used, He would use something else... It is not that God cannot be God without us, it is that we cannot be what He intended us to be without Him – without His Spirit.

So many people have been titillated and seduced by religion, but they have never understood who they really are or their purpose. When they join a church or get saved, often they do not realize that the transcendent Holiness of the God they worship actually comes to live in them, and whatever they are going through, they are bigger than the circumstances because the One who resides in them is the Creator of the world. God's Spirit that moved upon the face of the waters is expressed when we speak to one another kindly, compassionately and with mercy. But in order for us to talk like that we have got to first think like that.

Notice some of the things God has said about the importance of thinking right: *As a man thinketh in his heart so is he... Let this mind be in you that was also in Christ Jesus...: whatsoever things are lovely, pure, just, and of good report think on these things... be not conformed to this world but be transformed by the renewing of your mind... let this mind be in you that was also in Christ Jesus.* He is saying to us, in no uncertain terms, these are the things I want you to think about because I want you speak them. If you speak them then you are expressing God's Spirit in you and thereby renewing your mind and ultimately becoming a transformed person. Dr. King called this kind of person "a transformed non-conformant."

To find out who we really are, we must first take off our robe of flesh. We are God's Spirit in clothing. When we worship Him, we have to worship as one spirit to another Spirit. We cannot worship Him in the flesh, only in spirit and in truth. In addition, we have to worship as a speaking spirit. I really believe when we worship, we are going to draw spiritual warfare. Therefore, we must be on guard. We have to learn how to speak the Word of God as we worship because the enemy knows that we are worshipping and the one thing he does not want us to do is worship! He knows that if we worship, our strength will come, and when our strength begins to come we will begin to act like the One who made us. Then we will start talking and walking like Him. The fact is the enemy wants to keep us a captive of fear. His goal is to confine us to small thinking, but the moment we break through and understand that we are bigger than our circumstances, sicknesses, bills, heartaches and doubts – then we have victory.

In being godlike, we are supposed to look, think and move like the One true and living God as expressed in Jesus of Nazareth. When we do, we can say to an obstacle, "Be ye moved," and it will jump at God's command because it is no longer us saying it, but it is the much more powerful Holy Spirit saying it. My worship, witness, and work all operate out of who I really am. When I want things to move, I open my mouth to the Lord in faith and refuse to turn back.

The fact is the enemy wants to keep us a captive of fear. His goal is to confine us to small thinking, but the

moment we break through and understand that we are bigger than our circumstances, sicknesses, bills, heartaches and doubts – then we have victory.

THE QUIET STORM

I can recall the story of the storm that arose when Jesus and his Disciples were sailing across the Sea of Galilee. It had been a long day of preaching and healing work, and Jesus was exhausted. The wind howled and waves poured into the ship, threatening to sink it. When it appeared as though they would be lost, the disciples turned to Jesus, who was sleeping in the rear part of the craft. *And His disciples came to Him, and awoke Him, saying, Lord, save us: we perish. And He saith unto them, Why are ye fearful, O ye of little faith? Then He arose, and rebuked the winds and the sea; and there was a great calm* (Matthew 8:25-26).

When you want to quiet the storms in your life, speak to them in the Holy Spirit and with faith. When you open your mouth in this manner, demons tremble. If you express His Spirit in your home, everybody in your house will have to bow down, not to you but to the God in you. When you get His Spirit operating on the inside of you, you cannot walk into a college or university like any other student. There is a good chance that the professor himself will eventually recognize there is something about you that is compelling, powerful and magnetic.

Here is a challenge. I dare you to go on your job with a different attitude – the attitude of Him who lives in you. Even your boss will recognize that there is something different about you, that you are operating in authority. Try operating in authority of the Holy Spirit when creditors call to worry you about bills. Do not fuss with them out of the flesh. Understand that you are spirit, and speak to them out of the power that lives in you. You will see an amazing change. You will have to pay your bills, true enough, but speaking in the Spirit to those creditors will change both you and them because you will be operating in divine power.

Now, you will not understand how to operate out of the Spirit until you practice it daily. When this happens, you will automatically deal with trouble in a new way. It is not that trouble will disappear it will just bow down before you. You will become the victor and tell trouble what to do, not the other way around. When you master this lesson, you can overcome difficulties, including but not limited to death, sickness, poverty, chaos, worry and whatever else comes your way. Instead of debt dictating to you what your budget will be, you will begin telling debt what to do. When you do this, you can start expecting to receive checks instead of just writing them for bills.

When you want to quiet the storms in your life, speak to them in the Holy Spirit and with faith. When you open your mouth in this manner, demons tremble.

"Let a man cease from his sinful thoughts, and all the world will soften towards him, and be ready to help him," wrote James Allen. "Let him put away his weakly and sickly thoughts, and the opportunities will spring up on every hand to aid his strong resolves. Let him encourage good thoughts, and no hard fate shall bind him down to wretchedness and shame."

Worry is just a negative form of meditation. But if you could get yourself to understand who He is, you could saunter into the doctor's office recognizing that you have got something down on the inside of you that is bigger and better than any negative medical report. You could walk in and out of hospitals with a sense of confidence. When you opened your mouth in faith, difficulties would diminish, dilemmas would be deflated and all things would be possible to you. The New Testament offers stark evidence of what happened when Jesus spoke. He told people that it was not Him, but it was God working in Him that brought about miracles. When Jesus spoke, a crippled man walked, a dead girl rose up from her deathbed and Lazarus came out of the tomb. The same power is available to us. It is available when we speak words of faith believing God can do anything but fail, and we can overcome any obstacle.

Once you realize that you are a speaking spirit, you can start speaking what He has put in you. You can say *No weapon formed against me shall prosper* (Isaiah 54:17), or *the Lord is my shepherd; I shall not want* (Psalm 23:1); or *my God shall supply all of my needs according to his riches in glory by Jesus Christ* (Philippians 4:19); or *God gives us the power to get wealth* (Deuteronomy 8:18), or you can declare *I am healed by his stripes* (Isaiah 53:5)! These words constitute right thinking and will turn your world upside down and then right side up.

It is awesome when we think and speak about the goodness that the Bible says is the Spirit of Christ. If we can develop that Spirit in us, it will quicken our spirit, add years to our earthly life and give us unspeakable joy. I just want people to have everything that God has promised them. Our eternal life is connected to His Spirit. When we realize who we really are, it will cut down on the foolishness in our speaking. We will know then, that if it is not *love* we are expressing, it is not *Him*. If we talk thoughtlessly and inconsiderately, we will know it is not God. If we act irrational, it will be clear to us it is not the Lord. If our expression is mean-spirited, that cannot be Him. If we go to church and smile on Sunday but raise cane the following day, we may rest assured it is not Him. If our behavior is perfect at church, but nobody can stand living with us all week, you guessed it – it's not Him.

When Jesus spoke, a crippled man walked, a dead girl rose up from her deathbed and Lazarus came out of the tomb. The same power is available to us. It is available when we speak words of faith believing

God can do anything but fail and we can overcome any obstacle.

You have got to take time to reflect, meditate upon, and embrace His spirit. Ask God to help you express that Spirit in everything you do. If you do, I promise you that your frustrations will fade and the demons will be ditched. Get into that flow every day. Replace your words with the Word of God, and constantly remind yourself who you really are – a speaking spirit created to express love in everything you say and do. Welcome to the world of speaking spirits.

Chapter 6
Treasure Chest

'But we have this treasure in earthen vessels...'
– 2 Corinthians 4:7

She was pregnant at age 16, a high school dropout, and functionally illiterate. High Point, North Carolina, teen-age mother Fantasia Barrino made it through the first round of the American Idol contest with no problem, but when she showed up at the Georgia Dome in Atlanta for the next round, she was told by guards to go home because all of the audition spots were filled. Barrino could not believe it. She was in danger of missing out on potentially the biggest break of her young life. After all, she had been singing in church since age 5, and grew up performing and touring the southeastern United States with her family's gospel group, "The Barrino Family." Dejected and discouraged, she left the dome and contacted her dad, who sympathized with her plight but encouraged her to go back and try again. When she did, a security guard, who had been impressed when he heard her sing earlier, helped her sneak in. The rest is history.

Fantasia Barrino subsequently was named the 2004 American Idol and became an instant musical celebrity. The bare-footed, ninth-grade dropout achieved things that had once seemed impossible. Her debut album,

"Free Yourself," immediately went platinum, and her first single, "I believe," debuted at Number 1. A movie about her life called "Life Is Not A Fairy Tale: The Fantasia Barrino Story" followed, and she most excellently played the leading role in the hit Broadway play "The Color Purple." But it almost did not happen. Music fans all over the world nearly missed out on the treasure in Fantasia's chest – her soulful voice. That treasure was always inside of her, it just had to be brought out for everybody to hear and enjoy.

But we have this treasure in earthen vessels, that the excellency of the power may be of God, and not of us. We are troubled on every side, yet not distressed; we are perplexed, but not in despair; Persecuted, but not forsaken; cast down, but not destroyed; Always bearing about in the body the dying of the Lord Jesus, that the life also of Jesus might be made manifest in our body. For we which live are always delivered unto death for Jesus' sake, that the life also of Jesus might be made manifest in our mortal flesh. So then death worketh in us, but life in you (2 Corinthians 4:7-12). Listen to Eugene Peterson's biblical translation of this: *If you only look at us, you might well miss the brightness. We carry this precious Message around in the unadorned clay pots of our ordinary lives. That's to prevent anyone from confusing God's incomparable power with us. As it is, there's not much chance of that. You know for yourselves that we're not much to look at. We've been surrounded and battered by troubles, but we're not demoralized; we're not sure what to do, but we know that God knows what to do; we've been spiritually terrorized, but God hasn't left our side; we've been thrown down, but we haven't broken. What they did to Jesus, they do to us – trial and torture, mockery and murder; what Jesus did among them, He does in us – He lives! Our lives are at constant risk for Jesus' sake, which makes Jesus' life all the more evident in us. While we're going through the worst, you're getting in on the best!*

Fantasia learned to trust God despite the difficult circumstances that always seemed to be against her. She was wise to press ahead in faith. I, too, have learned the same lesson. I can assure you that without God my life would be nothing. As the song writer said: *Without Him I would fail. In fact, I would be like a ship without a sail.* As we say in the pulpit, God is the source of my strength. He is a doctor in a sick room, a lawyer in a courtroom and my walking stick when I get tired. He is my joy in sorrow and my hope for tomorrow. Simply put, without Him it would be difficult to achieve anything. If He had not found, saved, raised, healed, and helped me, where on earth would I be? Because of the treasure that each of have within us, it makes us indestructible and undefeatable.

It would not have been much of a contest if those American Idol producers would have only considered the outside of the contestants and not given them a chance to reveal their golden voices on the inside. As I have said, when you uncover your purpose you discover your power. But it is impossible to do what you are called to do without knowing your identity. If you see yourself as only a body, a vessel, or a clay pot, then you are always subject to the fate of the fragile, which is *broke, busted and disgusted* over the delicate nature of your existence. Call it what you will, a box, vessel, basket or chest, we have become preoccupied with self. We have forgotten that there is a blessing in the box, victory in the vessel, and a treasure in the trunk. How do we correct this misperception about the body we have? One way is by asking God to forgive us for putting too much attention on the vessel and not enough on the victory that He has placed in us – the same victory that He put in Fantasia Barrino, LeBron James, Bill Gates, Oprah Winfrey, John H. Johnson, Jordin Sparks and Barak Obama, not to mention other successful people.

If you see yourself as only a body, a vessel, or a clay pot, then you are always subject to the fate of the fragile, which is *broke, busted and disgusted* over the delicate nature of your existence. Call it what you will, a box, vessel, basket or chest. We have become preoccupied with self. We have forgotten that there is a blessing in the box, victory in the vessel, and a treasure in the trunk.

Although most people see themselves as just being a mere container, they do not understand who they really are. For example, many people worry too much about their financial condition and health. "Too often, we cry to Jesus to heal us, to take care of our finances, or to deliver us from problems, but we don't fully expect the good things to happen," wrote Joyce Meyer in her *Battlefield of the Mind* devotional. "We allow our minds to focus on the negative aspects. Doubt and unbelief war against our minds and steal our faith if we allow it." In other words, people are far too concerned about the bodies in which they live. In reality, as a spiritual treasure we are unstoppable, undefeatable, and unshakable. We become bigger and better than our container. The container may corrode, but there is no corruption in the cache. How we define ourselves becomes critically important in terms of our destiny. If I just saw myself as one who came up from slavery, but did not see myself as one who came down from a kingdom, then my whole perspective would be as the son of a slave instead of the child of a king.

When I tell you that you are not just a vessel, container or a box, I am not just making it up. As a matter of record, you are treasure in a chest! More precisely, you are a walking, talking, speaking treasure more valuable than you could ever have dreamed possible. When you speak out of His Spirit, you can expect to see the results that go along with that. You are in fact a treasure and guess what? Other people who speak from God's Spirit are no different. Every day think of yourself as a treasure in a vessel, not just as plain flesh and blood. Tell yourself that you are not just makeup, weave and concealer, but treasure. The Bible teaches us that God did it that way so as not to confuse the container with the content. Plain and simple, you are more than a container – much more. Bible scripture says the excellency is of God and not of us (2 Corinthians 4:7). This means this life is not about us; it is about Him who lives in us. It is about the treasure, as a matter of fact the "I AM" that resides in us.

How we define ourselves becomes critically important in terms of our destiny. If I just saw myself as one who came up from slavery, but did not see myself as one who came down from a kingdom, then my whole perspective would be as the son of a slave instead of the child of a king.

What? know ye not that your body is the temple of the Holy Ghost which is in you, which ye have of God, and ye are not your own? For ye are bought with a price: therefore glorify God in your body, and in your spirit, which are God's. (I Corinthians 6:19-20). When we become treasure, we will not be inclined to talk like trash, give like trash, and certainly not walk like trash because the treasure inside of us changes our vocabulary and sharpens our sense of victory. The Bible says as a man thinketh in his heart so is he. If my heart is a treasure then I will speak help and hope, not hurt and hogwash. *You realize, don't you, that you are the temple of God, and God Himself is present in you?* (1 Corinthians 3:16).

HIDDEN TREASURE

Not long ago, we were discussing domestic violence on my weekly radio show. The Bureau of Justice Statistics had reported that there were more than 560,000 intimate partner victimizations in this country annually. Even worse, domestic homicides against women continue to rise. On average, four women are murdered every day by their husbands or boyfriends in the U.S., and eight children are killed daily, as well, most often by a family member. Most victims of intimate-partner violence are women. Young women ages 20 to 24 are at greatest risk. From 2001 to 2005, children lived in households that experienced 38 percent of the intimate-partner violence incidents involving female victims. Those same children are 1,500 percent more likely to become victims themselves. The discussion on the radio show centered on how to survive the aggressive behavior of a person you love who simply wants to control and dominate you. We talked about verbal, psychological and physical abuse and how to deal with them. The answer is you certainly cannot handle those situations in the flesh. The best way to respond is in the spirit.

It is critical for us to believe there is a treasure in us. When we do, we should speak out of that treasure, especially in response to verbal abuse. When you are assaulted verbally, you must learn to talk out of your treasure instead of transmitting trash. Tell the abuser, "You will not bring me down to your level. When you are livid, I am going to show love. When you become animated, I am going to be accommodating, and if you curse me I am going to be calm because I am speaking out of a treasure." I'm not naïve about the difficulty of doing this, but it is our only hope. It is not easy for people to survive abusive situations, but when they have the Holy Spirit living inside of them, then they have a mighty powerful ally. Whatever difficulty you are facing, it is important to understand that you are not your own, you are God's child. Because your body and spirit belong to Him, you cannot just do with them whatever you feel like doing. How do you talk to your wife, your husband, or your child? Do you speak out of your treasure? What is your dialogue with those who persecute you? Does it emanate from your fortune or your failure? Jesus said, *Love your enemies, bless them that curse you, do good to them that hate you, and pray for them which despitefully use you, and persecute you* (Matthew 5:44). Dr. King said: "And there is still a voice saying to every potential Peter, 'Put up your sword.' History is replete with the bleached bones of nations. History is cluttered with the wreckage of communities that failed to follow this command. And isn't it marvelous to have a method of struggle where it is possible to stand up against an unjust system, fight it with all of your might, never accept it, and yet not stoop to violence and hatred in the process? This is what we have."

It is critical for us to believe there is a treasure in us. When we do, we should speak out of that treasure, especially in response to verbal abuse. When you are assaulted verbally, you must learn to talk out of your treasure instead of transmitting trash. Tell the abuser, "You will not bring me down to your level. When you are livid, I am going to show love. When you become animated, I am going to be accommodating, and if you curse me I am going to be calm because I am speaking out of a treasure."

I strongly encourage you to walk in that kind of power by understanding that you are more than a vessel. It is well established in God's Word that you are a treasure in the chest. Paul wrote to the Galatians, *I am crucified with Christ: nevertheless I live; yet not I, but Christ liveth in me: and the life which I now live in the flesh I live by the faith of the Son of God, who loved me, and gave himself for me* (Galatians 2:20).

As I have indicated before, words are so powerful because in them is life or death. Dr. Robert Schuller wrote in his classic *Tough Times Never Last, But Tough People Do!* "Positive words inspire positive emotions: humor, courage, optimism, faith, confidence. Whereas negative words stimulate negative emotions: suspicion, fear, distress, anger, doubt, depression, sadness, worry, jealousy."

The message of 1 Corinthians 6:19, which tells us that our bodies are temples of the Holy Spirit, not only means that we cannot live any way we please, it also implies that the people of God see us as we really are. We cannot dress or talk any kind of way because our whole body belongs to God. For instance, we cannot make nice to our brothers and sisters at church on Sunday and then use another kind of vocabulary on Monday. People are watching to see if what we say matches our actions. In spite of how we act in public, they will soon know what the real deal is because what is on the outside of us reflects what is inside. It has been said, "You can fool some of the people all of the time, and all of the people some of the time, but you can't fool all of the people all of the time."

CONTENT MATTERS

Everything that you are, God made you. Everything you have, He gave you. Therefore, when you move, live, and have your being in Him, in actuality it is the Father speaking and acting through you. Can you imagine how the world would be different if people really understood this? Racism and sexism could not stand if more people lived out of their treasure. Our world has been scarred by racism and sexism because people are looking at the vessel and not the victory. They are sizing up the container and not the content. Dr. King expressed in his "Dream" that we would all be judged not "by the color of our skin but by the content of our character."

If people in powerful positions had been looking at the treasure instead of the container, we would not have seen a difference in the response to the bridge collapse in Minneapolis, Minnesota, compared to the catastrophe in the Lower Ninth Ward of New Orleans, Louisiana, following Hurricane Katrina. The I-35W Bridge over the Mississippi River in Minneapolis collapsed during rush hour on August 1, 2007, plunging dozens of vehicles into the water. At least 13 people died and some 100 were injured. High ranking U.S. leaders, including President George W. Bush, First Lady Laura Bush, the Secretary of Transportation, several Congressional Representatives, and the national news media traveled to the wrecked bridge during the rescue and recovery operations. That was a good and decent thing for them to do. In contrast, much of New Orleans' Lower Ninth Ward experienced calamitous flooding from Katrina's storm surge in August of 2005. However, in the aftermath of the storm, President Bush and the federal government were heavily and rightly criticized for their slow response to one of the worse national disasters in history. Katrina cost the lives of at least 1,836 people and caused more than $81.2 billion in damage. If leaders had been operating out of their treasure, everybody involved, in both disasters, would have received the same treatment. The politicians have pledged to quickly rebuild the fallen bridge but that is Minneapolis, not the Lower Ninth Ward of New Orleans, where it will take decades to rebuild – if it happens at all. We see these inconsistencies occur because people, in high places, are looking at the container not the content.

Our world has been scarred by racism and sexism because people are looking at the vessel and not the victory. They are sizing up the container and not the content. Dr. King expressed in his "Dream" that we would all be judged not "by the color of our skin but by the content of our character."

According to the Word of God, we are not only a treasure but imperishable and cannot be defeated because of the power of God working in us. More than anything else, that is the victory we have. The victory is *in* the vessel, which is subject to the laws of nature but the treasure is not. The reason that we can say, "I am blessed and not distressed, I am healed and not sick, I am rich and not poor," is not because of the container, it is because of the content within the container. When we reach the place in life where we can define ourselves by our content, we have no hesitation in saying, "I am troubled but not taken out, I am distressed but not defeated, I am perplexed but not put down, I am persecuted but not put out, and I am cast down but not downcast. I was born in the ghetto but I have not allowed the ghetto to be born in me."

Biblical scripture says greater is He who is in me than he who is in the world (1 John 4:4). It says no weapon formed against me shall prosper (Isaiah 54:17). The scripture also says I can do all things through Christ who strengthens me (Philippians 4:13). If you speak from the treasure and live from the treasure, there is nothing that you will not be able to accomplish. We are overcomers but have not been overcome. The truth is that we are over the top and not under the bottom. We are unshakable and unmistakably His. We have immutable power way down on the inside of us. We are the seed of Abraham.

The reason that we can say, "I am blessed and not distressed, I am healed and not sick, I am rich and not poor" is not because of the container, it is because of the content within the container. When we reach the place in life where we can define ourselves by our content, we have no hesitation in saying, "I am troubled but not taken out, I am distressed but not defeated, I am perplexed but not put down, I am persecuted but not put out, and I am cast down but not downcast. I was born in the ghetto but I have not allowed the ghetto to be born in me."

I am a treasure because the "I AM" is within me! In looking at the story of Jesus' crucifixion, I can identify with His wounds, hurt and incredible suffering. When He hurts because of the way people act, believe it or not, I hurt. Bible scripture clearly teaches that because He was persecuted, we will be persecuted. *These things I have spoken unto you, that in Me ye might have peace. In the world ye shall have tribulation: but be of good cheer; I have overcome the world* (John 16:33). If we suffer with Jesus, we will also reign with Jesus. If we are put down with Jesus, we will also go up with Jesus. Our vessel might die, but our treasure will live forever. No matter how somebody might try, they won't be able to defeat or destroy it. Our treasure is irreproachable. As we say from the pulpit, bullets cannot shoot it, bombs cannot obliterate it, and rising tides cannot flood it.

I, like many of us, have tried to practice what I preach. I have often said from the pulpit, you can talk about me all you want, but I will still love you. Go ahead, lie on me, but I will still lift you. You may persecute me if you choose, but I will still be your friend. If it is your decision to kill me with your words, I will come back and bless you. How else could I have taken what came my way unless I knew, beyond a shadow of a doubt, that I was a treasure? There simply would have been no other way I could have made it. I am sure the same holds true for you, too.

If you accept the fact that you are treasure, you will never look at yourself the same way again. Again, as I often say on Sunday morning, you will put your shoulders back, head up, a glide in your stride, and pep in your step because you are a treasure of wonderful riches – of greater value than any one that the Pirates of the Caribbean could dig up. You have got something the world cannot take away. It is called joy and it is better than the most advanced medicine on the market. It is worth more than anything you can swallow, snort or inhale. Make no mistake about it, if we believe this, the victory is already ours. The victory is in Jesus. This is the truth that we must teach our children and grandchildren: It makes a big difference how we define ourselves, for far too many of us have low self-esteem because we do not know who we really are. Show your children and grandchildren the treasure inside of them and watch what happens next.

I, like many of us, have tried to practice what I preach. I have often said from the pulpit, you can talk about me all you want, but I will still love you. Go ahead, lie on me, but I will still lift you. You may persecute me if you choose, but I will still be your friend. If it is your decision to kill me with your words, I will come back and bless you. How else could I have taken what came my way unless I knew, beyond a shadow of a doubt, that I was a treasure? There simply would have been no other way I could have made it. I am sure the same holds true for you, too.

We live in a world that plays games with our minds. It seeks to make us sick and sad so that we are compelled to buy its products that will make us "well" and "happy." To counter this, we must learn to live out of our treasure. The phrase "don't worry be happy," as simplistic as that sounds is a call to live from the inside out and not the outside in. It is a call to live from the treasure and not the chest. Why worry about things, anyway? Because so many of us are focusing on the flesh, the devil has us walking in fear instead of faith. I like the saying when it is too hard to stand then it is time to kneel.

When the Apostle Paul said, *Oh death, where is thy sting? Oh grave, where is thy victory?* (1 Corinthians 15:55), he was speaking of what the biblical scriptures call the last enemy. When you live out of your treasure, even that enemy becomes your friend. Because the Bible says to be absent from the body is to be present with the Lord (2 Corinthians 5:8). It doesn't get any better than that.

Chapter 7
Renewing Your Mind

'And be not conformed to this world: but be ye transformed by the renewing of your mind, that ye may prove what is that good, and acceptable, and perfect, will of God.' – Romans 12:2

There is a story that I often tell about a little boy who kept falling out of bed. Sometime after the boy turned in each night, his mother would hear something go thump. She would then go into her son's room and sure enough, she discovered that he had fallen to the floor. One night, she came into his bedroom and told him that she was afraid he would hurt himself if he kept falling out of the bed. The boy was puzzled by his inability to stay in the bed and asked his mother why this happened every night as soon as he went to sleep. She told him that his problem was he was falling asleep too close to where he got in.

It is apparent to me that the problem many Christians are facing today is we have fallen fast asleep too close to where we got in the faith. The little boy, who kept falling out of the bed, did so because he chose to sleep near its edge. It would have been safer for him to sleep towards the middle of the bed. We are not getting all of what God wants for us because we are satisfied just to be saved instead of positioning ourselves in the center of God's will, which is being in the center of God's Word, or living by the wisdom of the Holy Bible. We can only do that if we learn to think right. And we won't learn how to think right unless we begin the process of renewing our minds. Paul Bourge said, "Unhappiness indicates wrong thinking, just as ill health indicates a bad regimen."

It is apparent to me that the problem many Christians are facing today is we have fallen fast asleep too close to where we got in the faith.

Let me paraphrase the Bible story about the lame man at the pool at Bethesda, a man that had suffered an infirmity for 38 years. As the account goes, hundreds of sick people, including the blind, crippled and paralyzed, would hang around the pool in hopes of being the first person to enter the water after it was touched by an angel, so they could be miraculously healed. When Jesus saw the lame man lying there, he asked him one question: "Do you want to get well?" The invalid responded by complaining to Jesus that every time he was ready to get into the pool at the critical moment, someone would beat him to the water. Jesus then gave him a simple commandment: *Get up, take your bedroll, start walking.* The lame man did as he was directed and instantly received his healing (John 5:2-9)

The key to the story, about the lame man at Bethesda, was when Jesus asked him if he wanted to get well. Do you know why that question was critical? Most people will say they want to be *healed* but what they really want is just to be *helped*. Novelist Thomas Wolfe said, "Most of the time we think we are sick, it's all in the mind." If that is all we want, then our lives are not going to change. No matter what obstacles that people are facing, if they have a renewed mind, God will help them to help themselves by His tender mercies. And the only way that we can get a renewed mind is to change our thinking. *I beseech you therefore, brethren, by the mercies of God, that ye present your bodies a living sacrifice, holy, acceptable unto God, which is your reasonable service. And be not conformed to this world: but be ye transformed by the renewing of your mind, that ye may prove what is that good, and acceptable, and perfect, will of God* (Romans 12:1-2).

A while ago, I saw a documentary called "Rize." It was a film about a dance expression born on the streets of South Central Los Angeles, California, that developed into cultural movement that came to be known as "Krumping." The documentary chronicled the movement's roots, which were in a dance representation called "clowning." Instead of being called Rize, actually, the movie should have been called "Fall." That is because it depicted a slice of a subculture that does not represent the best in us. Krumping and that whole lifestyle of gangbanging of the kind that has been exhibited by the Crips and Bloods gangs, is very real. When I saw the film, I said, "What were they thinking? These negative aspects of the hip-hop lifestyle have too much of a hold on the minds of our young people." Anyone who has seen the documentary would have to have said to themselves, "What *in the heaven* are they thinking?"

This movie makes an excellent case for why we need to pay more attention to renewing our minds. I have never seen more of a need for an entire people, the American people, Black people, White people, brown people and all of the shades of the rainbow, to renew our minds. To put it in other words, we need a mind overhaul. Not one that is just made over but a new mind. When I watched Rize, what I saw on the screen was a twisted presentation. I assure you that this is not what God wants. All across this land, there are different degrees of this sort of cultural expression everywhere we look. We must not accept them. Our goal must be to take our children back. This process has to begin with the renewing of our minds. This is not a call for a *redo* as much as it is for something brand new. It is not a reformation but a *trans*formation. The Latin prefix of "trans" means that it crosses every area of our lives. For example, we do not simply rearrange the furniture in our living room, but we exchange that furniture for a whole new set. Even though our spirits have been reborn through salvation, our minds – which is the seat of our emotions, will and intellect – must be renewed every single day of our lives. That is why it is possible for people to be saved and still live in defeat because they do not realize that even though God redeems the spirit, by faith we must change the flesh by working on it every day. In other words, faith without works is dead (James 2:20).

Our goal must be to take our children back. This process has to begin with the renewing of our minds. This is not a call for a *redo* as much as it is for something brand new. It is not a reformation but a *trans*formation.

SALVATION AND SANCTIFICATION

As I indicated above, the huge deception in the body of Christ is that all you have to do is be saved and leave it at that. Many people are literally lying down on their salvation. As a result, they cannot prosper or succeed because they are falling asleep too close to where they got in, like the little boy in my initial illustration. Although it is assured that we will go to heaven through salvation, so many of us needlessly catch hell right here on earth. When Jesus said in John 10:10: *I came so they can have real and eternal life, more and better life than they ever dreamed of,* I have a pretty good idea of what He had in mind. He was offering us a little bit of heaven on earth. It can never become a reality for the people of God as long as they sit on their salvation near the edge. It is such a wonderful thing to be going to heaven. I am so thankful and grateful to God that I am saved! But I figured out something a long time ago. If I want everything God has for me not only in heaven but right here on earth, I am going to have to do something to make sure I get all that He wants for me. Salvation will ensure a secure eternal life, but it requires sanctification. And sanctification does not mean belonging to a particular denomination. It does not mean we have to go to a certain church just because it is called a sanctified church. The people of God need to be sanctified, which means to be holy and to be holy means to be set apart. It does not mean to be conformed to the world but to be *transformed by the renewing of your mind* (Romans 12:2). There is a distinct difference between salvation and sanctification. To be sanctified is to work out our soul salvation. It is a minute by minute, moment by moment dying to self. It means that when someone steps on our toe or cuts us off in traffic or says something upsetting to us or makes us miserable, we have to die to self. When we are asked in church to give a larger than normal gift, we have to die to self not literally drop dead. Dying to self simply means surrendering our ego everyday, moment by moment. Once again we must understand what ego means. In short, it means *edging God out*. The apostle Paul said in Galatians 2:20: *I am crucified with Christ: nevertheless I live; yet not I, but Christ liveth in me: and the life which I now live in the flesh I live*

*by the faith of the Son of God, who loved me, and gave
Himself for me.*

**Although it is assured that we will go to heaven
through salvation, so many of us needlessly catch
hell right here on earth.**

Whether we realize or not, a healthy financial condition
comes from a healthy spiritual condition. Everything that
is visible was once invisible. Everything that is material
was once immaterial. In a real sense, money was first a
spirit. The people who wait on their employment check
every week or line up at the food pantries would agree
that money is important in their lives. We certainly would
not think that money is not important when we do not
get a raise or a promotion that we believe we deserve. Let
us stop fooling ourselves; money is a blessing *from* God
and it is used to bless the people *of* God. Money does not
make us happy or sad. It is our spiritual understanding
of money that determines our disposition. It is possible
for a rich man to be sad and a poor man to be happy.
Money does not determine joy. That is why the poorest
of the poor can say what the hymn writer said: "Jesus
is the center of my joy." On the other hand, God does
not want us *broke, busted and disgusted.* If we are broke,
we recognize that it is temporary. We can change our
attitude towards our condition by renewing our minds.
As essayist Joseph Joubert has said so clearly, "Misery

is almost always the result of thinking." It has also been said, "It isn't our position but our disposition that makes us happy or unhappy."

Let us stop fooling ourselves, money is a blessing *from* God and it is used to bless the people *of* God. Money does not make us happy or sad. It is our spiritual understanding of money that determines our disposition. It is possible for a rich man to be sad and a poor man to be happy. Money does not determine joy.

In his book *Reposition Yourself: Living Life Without Limits*, Bishop T.D. Jakes wrote: "True prosperity doesn't come from the outside. It comes from within. It isn't just about money; it is about a relentless commitment to progress. Prosperity is more about having a balanced and centered life without losing control of what God has given you... Personal responsibility falls within the same purview as fulfilling our God-given potential."

PRESENT YOUR MIND

One of the chief reasons we do not have enough of what we need is because we won't offer God our minds. People, who are operating with a renewed mind, rarely lack for anything. When the Bible said in Romans 12:1 *present your bodies a living sacrifice, holy, acceptable unto God, which is our reasonable service,* too often we think that means just to be present. But there is a difference between being *present* and *presenting* ourselves. Everyone who attends church on Sunday morning or Wednesday evening is present. What will get the best results, however, is when we are not only *present* but also *presenting* our minds to the cleansing of the Word of God. In other words, offering our minds to the Spirit of God. The process is real easy to begin. Just say, "God take my mind and renew it because I cannot stop doing what I am doing without a new mind!"

The difference between being *present* and *presenting* is the difference between showing up for class just to be there and striving for an "A" grade. When we attempt to achieve excellence while going to school, we are committed to making the honor roll. We are committed to being a valedictorian, or excelling enough to be Phi Beta Kappa. We may not always reach it, but there is nothing wrong with being committed to it. Some of us just want to go to class and be checked off when attendance is taken, and that is why stuff never changes. The reason things never improve for us is because our minds have us coming to church to be present but we never do any presenting. The Bible says the best way for us to please God and make an "A" is to renew our minds. Ask any classroom teacher. If I wanted to get an "A" in class, I would try to sit in the front so I could see and hear everything the instructor does and says. I am not saying I would not get an "A" sitting in the back, but it would be more difficult to do from back there. There is something about students who sit in the front and on the edge of their seat. They get into a habit of going in early, and even though sometimes they do not know the answer, they still are in great position to raise their hands to get the answer. The teachers are usually impressed by their eagerness to learn, and by their consistency of doing their homework on time. The students that go to school early and are ready to learn, will get the teacher's attention. Students attract attention when they go to school late, but it is the wrong kind of attention. The same is true when we go to our jobs early. If we are trying to earn a promotion or raise, we would be smart to go into work early. This is how we win favor. After all, if we had to line up for some football, basketball, concert or theater tickets, we would go early.

People, who are operating with a renewed mind, rarely lack for anything… In his book *Reposition Yourself: Living Life Without Limits*, Bishop T.D. Jakes wrote: "True prosperity doesn't come from the outside. It comes from within. It isn't just about money; it is about a relentless commitment to progress. Prosperity is more about having a balanced and centered life without losing control of what God has given you… Personal responsibility falls within the same purview as fulfilling our God-given potential."

Picture me with headphones listening to my IPOD or CD player and putting God's Word in my mind. And when I go on sabbatical, my wife, Beverly, often says, "Are you listening to that again?" What I am often listening to is the Word of God, and thereby renewing my mind by exchanging the information of the world for the inspiration of the Word. I tell my people on Sunday morning, here is how too many of us think: We do not have time to go to the CD table after church to get copies of the sermon, but we have time to beat everybody else to the Golden Corral restaurant after church to eat catfish. Second of all, we go under the faulty assumption that purchasing a CD or a worship track will take something from us and make someone else rich. Instead, what we should be doing is trying to figure out how to get a copy of the powerful worship and word we had this morning and play it 50 times to ignite our faith.

There are reasons why people sit in the rear of the church. It is hard to go to sleep during service sitting in the front. Many times they just want to be seen as present and they are not really concerned about the message. It is difficult to miss the message sitting in the front. If we want to be *sanctified* and not just *saved*, God wants us to participate in our sanctification. That is why God said forsake not the assembling of yourselves, which makes church attendance a Holy requirement: *And let us consider one another to provoke unto love and to good works: Not forsaking the assembling of ourselves together, as the manner of some is; but exhorting one another: and so much the more, as ye see the day approaching* (Hebrews 10:24-25). When our minds are transformed, we will insist that we want to be where the fire is – up front. It would be a mistake to think that we can just go to church, on Sunday morning, without first having to do any homework. *Study to shew thyself approved unto God, a workman that needeth not to be ashamed, rightly dividing the word of truth* (2 Timothy 2:15). That is how we who are present are supposed to present ourselves. If God wanted to sanctify us by Himself, He could do it but He does not because He wants us to participate. *For God so loved the world, that He gave His only begotten Son, that whosoever believeth in Him should not perish, but have everlasting life* (John 3:16). The Father gave us the Son and the Son gave us His life. In other words, God did His part, the Son did His part and now we have to do our part.

How I wish I could just wave my hand and all the late goers to church would just stop going late. But if I could, some of them would just shrug it off, go back to their habitually tardy behavior and say, "I don't care what you say, I am going to do exactly what I have been doing. At least I am going to church, aren't I?" But don't you see, that is just being present and not being a presenter. And as a result, it means they are going to get exactly what they have been getting – because they are living too close to the edge. They are going to keep missing worship and getting in just in time for the sermon, still not understanding that it is in worship that we give ourselves to God. If our hearts are set on receiving an "A" in blessings, we need to get to church early and stay late. And while we are there, stay awake. If we have trouble staying awake because we worked too hard over the past week or were up too late the night before, we need to pick a seat next to a designated "poker." Tell that person if you fall asleep to just poke you in the side because although you are present, you do not want to miss anything.

The meaning of Romans 12:1 is that we should give ourselves as offerings, not just on Sunday but in our everyday lives. This includes our waking up and going to bed lives. It also means in our coming, going, working, playing and giving. God wants us to continually strive for an "A." Eugene Peterson wrote Romans 12:1 this way: *So here is what I want you to do, God helping you: Take your everyday ordinary life, your sleeping, your eating, your going to work, and your walking around life and place it before God as an offering. Embracing what God does for you is the best thing you can do for Him.*

God was saying through the story of the lame man lying by the pool at Bethesda that He is ready, willing and able to help us, but He first wants to know what we really want. Do we just want a healing, or do we want to be completely transformed? If we want to be transformed, then we need to pick up our beds and walk. We need to pick up our Bibles and study. We must pick up ourselves as an offering unto God. We should not blame God for our lack of success. It is not that God does not want to bless us. It is that we are not presenting our bodies and mind to Him for transformation. It is an attitude problem. You have heard it said that *attitude determines altitude*. The lame man at the pool is a perfect example. I like what Michael Hirsch, a person with AIDS, once said, "When people asked, I used to tell them how sick I was. The more I talked about being sick, the worse I got. Finally, I started saying, 'I am getting better.' It took a while, but then I started to feel better, too." If we desire to be sanctified, we are going to have to offer ourselves as sacrifices and become presenters instead of just being present. If we want to get off spiritual welfare, we are going to have to participate and not just take up space in the church or on the planet.

Chapter 8
'Man In The Mirror'

'I have a dream that my four little children will one day live in a nation where they will not be judged by the color of their skin, but by the content of their character.' – Dr. Martin Luther King Jr.

Many people remember Michael Jackson's blockbuster hit song called "Man in the Mirror." It was a popular refection of man's image. In other words, who do we see when we look in the mirror? Do we see color or character? Do we seen external or internal? Do we see flesh or spirit? Do we see problems or possibility? What do you see when you look at the man or woman in the mirror?

The chorus to Jackson's song goes, "I'm starting with the man in the mirror; I'm asking him to change his ways, and no message could have been any clearer; If you wanna make the world a better place, if you wanna make the world a better place; Take a look at yourself, and then make a change, Take a look at yourself, and then make a change... Na na na, na na na, na na, na nah..."

Have you ever asked yourself, "What is my purpose in life?" If so, I will give you a hint. You cannot answer that question by starting with yourself, you must begin with God, wrote Rick Warren in his bestselling book, *Purpose*

Driven Life: What On Earth Am I Here For? "It is only in God that we discover our origin, our identity, our meaning, our purpose, our significance, and our destiny. Every other path leads to a dead end," declared Warren. Many people spend their whole lives trying to determine the reason for their existence. They continually ask themselves why they were born and what they are supposed to do with their lives. Some would like to know about how long they will live. They continually grapple with decisions over where they should settle down, whether or not they should marry and what causes they will become involved with.

Throughout this book, I have been talking about the issue of right and wrong thinking. I have been making the case that if there is a wrong way of doing something, there also has to be a right way of doing it. A big part of who we are and what we do and how we function is based on theology, which represents what we think about God. What we think about God and who we think God is has everything to do with who we think we are.

A couple from our church clearly understood who they were when they recently went to purchase a house. When the man who was selling the property told them its list price, the couple indicated to him that they thought it cost too much. His response was, "Well, what would you like me to do about it?" The couple retorted, "First of all, we want you to know that the 'I AM' sent us." While we might be inclined to chuckle about their comment to the salesman, the eventual result was that he reduced the price of the house by $50,000. The details of a story like this sound so unreal that they seem almost unbelievable, but I can assure you that the principle this couple used to receive a huge financial blessing is based upon sound biblical doctrine. If we use this principle the way they did, it will change our lives. As a matter of fact, it will change our understanding of who we are and, most importantly, whose we are. In other words, we are a speaking spirit. We are the reflection of "I AM." When we speak in the authority of "I AM," things begin to happen and favor begins to flow towards us.

PURPOSE AND PASSION

When we see ourselves as the "I AM," we are not only representing the *image* of God, we are also declaring His purpose. And when we declare God's purpose, we also express His power. It is one thing to live our lives not knowing who we are, but our ignorance is compounded when we do not know why we were put here. Early twentieth century evangelist William A. "Billy" Sunday once said, "More men fail through lack of purpose than lack of talent." Likewise, 19th century Scottish essayist, satirist, and historian Thomas Carlyle, said, "A man without a goal is like a ship without a rudder."

Once we know our purpose, we must pursue it. When we do not understand our purpose, we live aimless, powerless, and pointless lives. The problem with too many people is their lives are going in no particular direction. In other words, they miss the mark of the Lord's high calling, which is basically what happens when they sin. No matter who we think we are, we have got to pursue our goals passionately. In other words, our purpose must be our focus. More folks have failed to reach their goals because of a lost purpose than for any other reason. The old saying is true, *if you don't know where you are going any road can take you there.* In his book *The Laws of Thinking*, Bishop E. Bernard Jordan said: "You must be in alignment of purpose with God if your actions are to bring forth the manifestations He desires."

An example of somebody who lost his purpose, and hence his focus, is fallen football star Michael Vick. A celebrated National Football League quarterback who was among the most gifted athletes to ever play the game, Vick was sentenced to 23 months in prison in 2007 for criminal conspiracy resulting from his involvement in felonious dog fighting. His troubles cost him a great deal. He had signed a $130 million contract with the Atlanta Falcons in 2004, making him the highest paid NFL player at the time, but the conviction caused him to lose much of that money. The case represents a classic misunderstanding, by a man, of what is his purpose. In retrospect, Michael Vick, who needs our prayers, is really no different than most of us. Sometimes we think we are better than the people who fall, but if we were honest we would have to admit that we have all made mistakes at times in our lives. All we can do is thank God that He picked up the broken pieces and allowed us to continue. In spite of our failures, we must learn to persevere. And like the songwriter says, "We fall down, but we get up." One of the keys to overcoming in life is when we get knocked down 9 times, we get back up 10.

It is incumbent upon young people today to realize that they have got to be very careful, not only about their focus but about with whom they chose to associate. I do not know much about Michael Vick's church or spiritual life, but I do know that he had some lousy associates. They were unreliable and disloyal to him when he needed them the most. His predicament is a warning to us that we had best watch with whom we hang out. I am not sure whether it was Vick or his associates that were more at fault. Because they were so close, it is difficult to tell which of them was responsible for doing what. Still, it is important for young people to understand that they begin to act like those around them. The primary reason that I came out of the world and entered the church is because I wanted to be around some people who were like Jesus. Parents who have children living at home need to be aware of their children's associates. Even if their children do not live with them, there will still be opportunities for parents to make an impact on with whom their children associate. A parent is still a parent no matter the age of their children. When parents see their child hooking up with the wrong folks, they would be wise to warn them about the potential trouble ahead.

Once again, in Michael Vick's case, here was a talented boy raised by an unwed mother. Vick's mother was 16-years-old when he was born. As I have said in a previous chapter, therein lies the danger of boys being raised in female-headed households. Again, this is not a putdown of the females because without them, we would have no existence, and without their love, we would have nothing at all. But again, it takes a man to show a boy how to be a man. This is not to say that there have not been many successful examples of young men raised by single-parent mothers or grandmothers. I was blessed to be raised by a single-parent grandmother. But I still maintain, as blessed as I was and as blessed as I am, my grandmother could not teach me to be something she was not. She was a great woman, a great provider but she was not a man. I wrote in my family-friendly book *The Home Alone Syndrome*, "What was once *nuclear* has now become *unclear*. Parents and children all seem to suffer from *role confusion*, each doing his or her own thing, with any semblance of discipline and personal responsibility fast going the way of the dinosaur. The African proverb is true to a fault: *A single bracelet does not jingle*. It takes more than one person to make a home and to make a difference. That goes for any relationship worthy of the name. Sadly, children who are left *home alone* are placed in the greatest jeopardy of all."

I wrote in my family-friendly book *The Home Alone Syndrome*, "What was once *nuclear* has now become *unclear*. Parents and children all seem to suffer from *role confusion*, each doing his or her own thing, with any semblance of discipline and personal responsibility fast going the way of the dinosaur. The African proverb is true to a fault: *A single bracelet does not jingle*. It takes more than one person to make a sound, to make a home, and to make a difference."

In contrast to Michael Vick's calamity, another top professional sports figure has been able to maintain focus in pursuit of his purpose for over 10 years. When Tiger Woods made a dramatic tournament winning 25-foot putt to win the Arnold Palmer Invitational by one shot in March of 2008, he notched his 64th career victory and fifth straight to tie the legendary Ben Hogan at number three on the Professional Golf Association Tour list. The magnificent shot earned Woods $1,044,000 and put him on the verge of earning $80 million for his young career. He had also won the Buick Invitational golf tournament in late January 2008, when the number one player in the world notched his 62nd career victory and tied Palmer for fourth place on the all-time PGA victory list in half the time. He is the youngest player ever to achieve the Career Grand Slam and the youngest and fastest to win 50 tournaments on tour. Woods followed up the Buick win with a spectacular victory at the Dubai Desert Classic of the United Arab Emirates in February 2008. "It's the ideal start, isn't it?" said Woods, who made up four strokes on the final day of the tournament to notch his second straight victory. He went on to win the U.S. Open with a torn ACL and a fractured knee thereby rising above his physical condition with the sheer power of his mind. "You play to win. So far, I've done that this year. My mind is my biggest asset," noted Woods, born in 1975. "I expect to win every tournament I play." Again this is proof positive that right thinking produces right results. Many people want to study Tiger Woods' golf game, but the key to his success is how he thinks. After all, isn't it all in your mind?

My mind is my biggest asset," noted Woods, born in 1975. "I expect to win every tournament I play." Again this is proof positive that right thinking produces right results. Many people want to study Tiger Woods' golf game but the key to his success is how he thinks. After all, isn't it all in your mind?

SOWING CARELESSLY

Getting back to our purpose, the Bible outlines precisely what that is in Genesis 1:28, when God told mankind to *Prosper! Reproduce! Fill Earth! Take charge.* That was a defining moment, where God actually laid out our purpose. That is why He made man. This scripture also declares that our purpose is to be fruitful not foolish, and it instructs us to multiply, subdue and replenish the earth, and take dominion over every living thing. There is a difference between dominion and destruction. People sometimes get confused about the two. It seems that we are destroying the earth in our own way. In Michael Vick's case, using dogs to destroy each other for selfish gain is outside of God's purpose. We were given charge and dominion over the animal kingdom, but that has nothing to do with maiming them or destroying them for personal gain or sport.

Even more importantly, God's instruction, to us, to multiply does not mean that we are to play loosey-goosey with the opposite sex. The key word here is responsibility. Women, your baby's daddy needs to be your husband. Men and boys, your baby's mother ought to be your wife. I do not care what kind of society we are living in today. I know that we are out of control, but somebody needs to ring the bell. Someone needs to stand up and sound the horn. Every young boy needs to recognize that he should not be scattering his seed recklessly all over the place – like straw blowing in the wind. When God said reproduce and fill the earth, He was not giving human beings permission for babies to have babies. Men and women need to sow their seeds responsibly in covenant relationships. It is called marriage *under God between a man and a woman and before these witnesses.*

The key word here is responsibility. Women, your baby's daddy needs to be your husband. Men and boys, your baby's mother ought to be your wife... I know we are out of control but somebody needs to ring the bell... Men and women need to sow their seeds responsibly in covenant relationships. It is called marriage *under God between a man and a woman and before these witnesses.*

According to a 2008 report on the state of Black youth compiled by Indiana Black Expo, 8 in 10 black youths were born to unwed mothers in 2007. The report also found that about 250,000 teens, between ages 15 and 19, become pregnant every year in the U.S. The report stated that, according to Indiana State Department of Health statistics, 30 percent of Indiana high school students were sexually active in '07. When God says multiply, He means to reproduce in His image. God wants us to take dominion over our world, but He first wants us to have a mental makeover. That is how we will recover from all of this baby's mama drama. We have to change the way we think. It is not alright or cute for young people to bring another human being into this world for whom they cannot give adequate care. The young father does not have a job; the young mother cannot support herself, and they are putting their parental responsibilities on mama – that's drama. Mama has already raised hers, now they want her to raise theirs.

Along with our purpose to reproduce, replenish and fill the earth, the purpose of our divinity is to be fruitful, meaning to bear the fruit of the Lord's Spirit. In other words, our purpose is to reflect the image of God. When we see ourselves in His image, it changes everything that we do. It changes our thought process, which means there are a lot of things we used to do that we cannot do anymore because we are not just anybody – we are a reflection of the Almighty God. In His image, we cannot steal, lie, fornicate or adulterate. If we do these things, then we simply are denying who we *really* are.

Many of our young people are hip to the pop song "Stunting Like My Daddy," which has sexually demeaning and grotesque lyrics. They should also know that they will have to go up to another level to understand where their real "Daddy" is. As the hymn writer says, we are our heavenly Father's children. If they are going to stunt or act like their daddy, it would be wise for them to stunt or act like the One who made them. I am speaking of the "I AM" in whose image we have all been made.

When our father and mother forsake us, there is still somebody who will lift us up (Psalm 27:10). When the Father lives in us, we are inclined to do everything differently. We will speak, act, and give differently than we did before. In fact, we become a reflection of God in everything we do. And that is not all. When we realize that we are the image of the Almighty, then we attract what the Almighty attracts. We do not have to worry about looking for love in all the wrong places because the "I AM" in us *is* love. There will be no need for us to stumble around in search of peace and joy because the "I AM" in us is peace and joy. Once we realize this and live by it, all things are ours.

According to a 2008 report on the state of black youth compiled by Indiana Black Expo, 8 in 10 black youths were born to unwed mothers in 2007... When God says multiply, He means to reproduce in His image. God wants us to take dominion over our world, but He first wants us to have a mental makeover. That is how we will recover from all of this baby's mama drama. We have to change the way we think. It is not alright or cute for young people to bring another human being into this world for whom they cannot give adequate care. The young father does not have a job; the young mother cannot support herself, and they are putting their parental responsibilities on mama – that's drama. Mama has already raised hers, now they want her to raise theirs.

POWER OF 'I AM'

As noted before, God called Himself the "I AM" (Exodus 3:14). In addition to standing for the Lord's image and purpose, the name also represents God's power. There is power in the name of "I AM." This is exactly what I and one of our church prison ministry teams, called MOD (Men of Discipline), reminded prisoners when we visited the reformatory at Pendleton, Indiana. We reminded them of the great "I AM" who lives in each one of us. As we neared the end of the 45-minute drive to the prison located a few miles northeast of Indianapolis, I was once again struck by the sprawling prison industrial complex. I did not see it as just another jailhouse. It was much more than that. The sobering, mammoth compound was comprised of acres of land, buildings and barbed-wire fences, which housed human potential that has been locked up and locked down. The towering walls incarcerated somebody's husband, father, brother, nephew, uncle and cousin, mostly as the result of poor choices and bad associa-tions. Just as in other states across the country, Indiana's prisons are overcrowded. Naturally, the problem has been compounded by politicians who have decided that it is easier to incarcerate than to educate those who are at the greatest risk of slipping into the justice system.

Let's face it, incarceration has become a business. Billions of dollars are made off of building prisons and supporting them. The leaders in my city and in this nation have bought into the philosophy that it is more prudent to lock them up rather than lift them up. However, we reminded the young men, who we shared our time with at Pendleton, that there is a way out regardless of whether they will be released soon or remain in prison for many years. We told them about the great "I AM," who takes up residence in each one of us. We informed them that even though they were in prison, the prison does not have to be in them. Our message to them was we are bigger than our circumstances, and He who dwells in us is not really subject to natural law. In other words, you can be locked up and still be free. We assured them that despite the fact that they have been convicted of crimes and were duly incarcerated, they are still human beings created in the image of the great "I AM," and created to fulfill His purpose on the earth. What a day that was. We prayed with them and asked them to continue spreading the "I AM" spirit throughout the reformatory.

We told them about the great "I AM," who takes up residence in each one of us. We informed them that even though they were in prison, the prison does not have to be in them. Our message to them was we are bigger than our circumstances, and He who dwells in us is not really subject to natural law. In other words, you can be locked up and still be free. We assured them that despite the fact that they have been convicted of crimes and were duly incarcerated, they are still human beings created in the image of the great "I AM," and created to fulfill His purpose on the earth. What a day that was. We prayed with them and asked them to continue spreading the "I AM" spirit throughout the reformatory.

It is interesting how everybody that is locked up is not in jail, while some of us who are free are actually in spiritual bondage. Some of the young men that we visited in prison are, in essence, still free. That is because they have "broken out" of prison by surrendering to the One who is able to keep them from falling and can present them before the throne of God without spot or blemish. That would be the great "I AM," whose power is described in Isaiah 41:10: *Don't panic. I'm with you. There's no need to fear for I'm your God. I'll give you strength. I'll help you. I'll hold you steady, keep a firm grip on you.* The power given to us is ordained by God. We have the responsibility to remind prisoners, politicians, and even preachers that their power comes from God. This point is underlined in Romans 13:1: *Let every soul be subject unto the higher powers. For there is no power but of God: the powers that be are ordained of God.*

I shall never forget what my friend, Dr. Adrian Rogers, the late renowned longtime pastor of Bellevue Baptist Church in Memphis, Tennessee, cautioned me about regarding the deception of success. He was warning a group of us younger preachers about the danger of arrogance. He said, "Tom, the higher you go up the totem pole, the more of your behind is showing." No matter how high people go up the totem pole, no matter how successful they become personally and professionally, Dr. Rogers reminded us that all power is still in God's hands. In other words, if the Lord God would decide to withdraw His hand from us, we would be nothing. *I am the vine, ye are the branches: He that abideth in Me, and I in him, the same bringeth forth much fruit: for without Me ye can do nothing.* (John 15:5).

The Bible says in Psalm 8:2 that we are strong in the Lord God: *Out of the mouth of babes and sucklings hast thou ordained strength because of thine enemies, that thou mightest still the enemy and the avenger.* God has given us the power to handle our enemies, assailants, would be assassins, and adversaries – especially the ones who attempt to blindside us. In other words, thankfully, God has our backs. If He had not ordained our strength from our mothers' wombs, we would not have made it this far. If it had not been for the Lord on our side, where would we be? I will tell you where we would be, we would be in a mess far greater than the one we are already in. We are reminded in 2 Timothy 1:7 that we *have not been given the spirit of fear but of power, love and a strong mind.* Clearly, the spirit that I am referring to, here, comes from the "I AM." The spirit we have is of power, love and right thinking. Having a strong mind means thinking right, but having a weak mind represents thinking wrong.

As the Bible says in Acts 1:8, after we have received baptism from the Holy Spirit, we are imbued with power! That power is not out there in the stratosphere somewhere, it is in us beginning when we first become believers in the Gospel of Jesus Christ. Unfortunately, there are a lot of people sitting in Christian churches today who are believers, but are not aware of how to exercise their power. They have no power because they have not surrendered their lives and allowed the Holy Spirit to come in and take charge of every part, portion, and parcel of their lives. The Bible says in Revelation 3:20: *Behold, I stand at the door, and knock: if any man hear my voice, and open the door, I will come in to him, and will sup with him, and he with Me.* If we allow the Holy Spirit to come in and commune with us, God will give us power like we have never known. If only we could get out of the rut of the ego-driven ways of doing things, and learn that we already possess more than adequate power to overcome any obstacles we face. The key is to figure out how to rest in, rule over, and lean on that power. This is critical knowledge that is never really understood by some intellectuals. *Isn't it obvious that God deliberately chose men and women that the culture overlooks and exploits and abuses, chose these 'nobodies' to expose the hollow pretensions of the 'somebodies'* (1 Corinthians 1:27-28)? The Bible also says the gospel is hid to them that are lost (2 Corinthians 4:3-4).

POWER IN THE NAME

For certain, the power of God lies in our use of His name. Ephesians 1:21 says God's name stands for *principality, power, might, dominion, and is a name above every name that is named, not only in this world, but also in that which is to come.* Act 4:12 declares: *For there is none other name under heaven given among men, whereby we must be saved.* The Word of God also says that demons tremble, the dead are raised, lions' jaws are locked, fires are quenched, and floods recede at the name of Jesus.

Besides the power in the *name* of Jesus, there is also power in His *blood* – the same blood of the Lamb who was slain and whose blood was shed for us on the cross. According to the Bible in Acts 20:28, the Church of God was purchased with the His own blood. Revelation 1:5 tells us that we were washed by the blood of Jesus, while Revelation 5:9-10 says: *And they sung a new song, saying, Thou art worthy to take the book, and to open the seals thereof: for Thou wast slain, and hast redeemed us to God by Thy blood out of every kindred, and tongue, and people, and nation. And hast made us unto our God kings and priests: and we shall reign on the earth.* Finally, Revelation 12:11 declares: we overcame the enemy *by the blood of the Lamb and by the word of our testimony.* As speaking spirits, we learn that we can overcome anything by what we say and by the blood of the Lamb. Because of this faith fact, no matter what we are dealing with and no matter what we have to go through, "We shall overcome."

Chapter 9
The Imago Dei

'When you and God become one, all of life's resources begin to flow towards you.' – Howard Thurman

Imagine, for a moment, that you could travel to anywhere in the world you want to go. Could you see yourself visiting Asia, Africa, Australia, Israel, Europe, South America or China? Suppose you could choose any house you wanted to live in, the model of your car or the amount of your income? I could just envision the typical responses that I would get from people who were not convinced they could ever enjoy such blessings:

"Traveling the world may be for some people but not me. I am too busy trying to make ends meet to travel," somebody would say.

"You've got to be kidding. No mortgage company, in its right mind, would qualify me to buy that home in a million years – dream on," another would say.

Still another would declare: "There's just no way… I have got too many obligations on me to risk setting aside some of my hard-earned money for any foolishness. Investing in securities or starting a business may be for some folks, but it is not for me. Give me a break."

Do these excuses sound familiar? Some folks are satisfied with just getting by. Others honestly believe that they are not supposed to have any more than the bare necessities of life. I have always been taught that you can have a little heaven on earth. My grandmother used to say that "It's not pie in the sky when you die bye and bye, but it is being sound on the ground while you are still around." It all depends on how we think about God. So much of our ability to walk in plenty or to languish in poverty has a great deal to do with how we think, or how our forefathers passed down thought patterns to us.

My grandmother used to say that "It's not pie in the sky when you die bye and bye, but it is being sound on the ground while you are still around."

When God told Moses to go down and deliver His people from the oppressive hand of the Egyptians, Moses wondered by whose authority he should tell the people of Israel that he had been sent: *Then Moses said to God, 'Suppose I go to the People of Israel and I tell them, "The God of your fathers sent me to you"; and they ask me, "What is His name?" What do I tell them?' God said to Moses, 'I-AM-**THAT**-I-AM. Tell the People of Israel, "I-AM sent me to you"* '(Exodus 3:13-14). [1]

---

[1] **(Scripture word in bold inserted from the King James Version)**

When Moses said the "I AM" had sent him, he was expressing the authority that he had been given and the power
to back it up. In the same way, when we say the "I AM"
is a part of us, what we are really doing is declaring our
purpose and expressing our power.

Traditional religion majors in recognizing the transcendent
God, who is the God outside of us, while it minors in the
imminent God, who is God inside of us. As a result, we
are often in a *wait and see* mode when it comes to doing
the work of God or acting on what we believe. It is as if
we are waiting on permission to be powerful. You do not
need permission to be powerful. If you know who you
are in the Master, you are already powerful!

**Then Moses said to God, 'Suppose I go to the People of
Israel and I tell them, "The God of your fathers sent me
to you"; and they ask me, "What is His name?" What
do I tell them?' God said to Moses, 'I-AM-THAT-I-AM.
Tell the People of Israel, "I-AM sent me to you"**

Whatever we are struggling and dealing with, whatever
problems and pain that we have self-inflicted, have
everything to do with the way we think. We have to
stop blaming others and outside circumstances for our
problems and begin to investigate the nature of our
thought process. If folks could only grasp the fact that the
Bible is so much more than a book of stories, we would
see more progress. Sometimes we, as believers, have

forgotten that we are baptized in the Holy Ghost. The Bible says so in the book of Acts: *Ye shall receive power, and after that the Holy Ghost comes upon you* (Acts 1:8). The seat of that power of which I speak is not sitting out there in some far away galaxy, it is inside of us.

So often, in the past, we have given away our power. There have been too many times that we did not get what we needed because we were waiting for God to get it for us when He has already given us the power to get it for ourselves. "Most people will agree with you when you begin to complain about the things around you that you think are controlling your life – whether it's the traffic that made you mad, the government who took your money, the boss who did you wrong or the spouse who keeps you upset," wrote Casey Treat in his book *Renewing the Mind*. "In reality, you are making choices about all these things. Your involvement with them and how you deal with them is determined by you."

The Bible teaches us that God is omnipotent, omniscient and omnipresent, which means He is all powerful, all knowing and is everywhere at the same time. Because God is everywhere, the Lord can be both outside and inside of us at the same time. In other words, divinity dwells in us. The God of Abraham, Isaac, Jacob, Moses, Daniel, Jonah, Joshua, Paul, Peter, and Stephen is in us. There is no bit of knowledge more important than this. We must be careful not to unknowingly give away our power and authority that we have received from the "I AM" God.

I say with a bit of sadness that teaching people how to become empowered is not emphasized by most seminaries or religious institutions, including churches. I am sure it is not true, but I sometimes wonder if there has not been some conspiracy by traditional religion to diminish our understanding of who we really are in Christ so that we would be dependent on religious institutions. God is great, good, strong, powerful, pure and holy. It is the same God who resides in us.

In *The Power of Positive Thinking*, Norman Vincent Peale wrote that an "effective technique in problem solving is the simple device of conceiving of God as a partner. One of the basic truths taught by the Bible is that God is with us. In fact, Christianity begins with that concept, for when Jesus Christ was born he was called Immanuel, meaning 'God with us.' "

The name "I AM" means the eternal unchangeable God. To put it another way, the "I AM" we are talking about represents a stable and all powerful spiritual alliance between us and God. God's perpetuity is a major facet of His personality. If I may phrase it succinctly from the scripture, Jesus Christ the same yesterday, and to day, and for ever (Hebrews 13:8). To use a Bible metaphor, even when you take away, mortify, destroy or kill the flesh, the "I AM" is all that will be left. I have said before that we who believe in Jesus are not "wannabes." We are not even a going-to-be. In essence, we are what God is, and God is what we are. To be specific, we are the "I AM." Ignorance tries to convince us not to refer to ourselves as the "I AM," because that takes something away from God. But just the opposite is true. When we believe that we are the "I AM," we are honoring God and accepting exactly who the Lord declares that we are.

In essence, we are what God is, and God is what we are. To be specific, we are the "I AM." Ignorance tries to convince us not to refer to ourselves as the "I AM," because that takes something away from God. But just the opposite is true. When we believe that we are the "I AM," we are honoring God and accepting exactly who the Lord declares that we are.

God said our temple, which is our body, is the temple of the "I AM." The lack of this knowledge greatly contributes to our dilemma as a people. Here we have been going around begging, stumbling, pathetic, and feeling sorry for ourselves without knowing that we were born to be supermen and superwomen. J.A. Rogers, in his essential book *From Superman to Man*, makes the point that the Black man has descended from an extraordinary superman to an ordinary man. Rogers was speaking of the Black man as a descendent of the kings and queens of Africa, but you can see how this applies to every man who sees himself as a spiritual descendent of King Jesus. And this makes every man royalty. *But ye are a chosen generation, a royal priesthood, an holy nation, a peculiar people; that ye should shew forth the praises of Him who hath called you out of darkness into His marvellous light* (1 Peter 2:9). Far too many followers of Jesus have fallen all the way down the mountain and become just ordinary, powerless creatures. Unfortunately, when we are in this condition, there is practically no evidence of divinity dwelling in us. The falling was caused by the way we think or the way we have been taught to think. You won't hear this truth being taught in too many of our traditional churches. This is why I believe we are still in bondage. Far too many teachers of faith will not step out beyond spiritual infancy, and they are keeping the people imprisoned. Do not accept it! Use the "I AM" power to get off of spiritual welfare. Stop depending on someone to always do something for you and start doing for yourself by operating in the power of God. Begin to get where you want to go by using the tremendous power you have been given from the "I AM" in you. A. L. Kitselman said it this way, "The words 'I AM…' are potent words; be careful what you hitch them to. The thing you're claiming has a way of reaching back and claiming you."

I believe we are still in bondage. Far too many teachers of faith will not step out beyond spiritual infancy, and they are keeping the people imprisoned. Do not accept it! Use the "I AM" power to get off spiritual

welfare. Stop depending on someone to always do something for you and start doing for yourself by operating in the power of God.

THE IMAGE OF POWER

In Genesis 1:27, the Bible describes how God made mankind: *So God created man in His own image, in the image of God created He him; male and female created He them.* Because all of us were made in God's image, we are showing our ignorance when we allow the devil to trick us into looking upon another human as being inferior. Females are not inferior to males as both are created in His image. Those with light skin color are not inferior to those with darker skin tones, and those with dark skin are not inferior to light-skinned people. Consider how Eugene Peterson interprets the same Genesis 1:27 verse: *God created human beings; He created them godlike, reflecting God's nature. He created them male and female.* I know that many people are afraid to say they are godlike because of religious tradition, but it is still true. When we look at God, His reflection should be in us, and when people look at us they should see this reflection.

Let me be clear, you are not God but you are godlike. In other words, you are not God, but you were made in His image. As a matter of fact, you are a speaking spirit in an earth suit. The power of God is in you and when you speak, something is supposed to happen. Acts 17:28 says:

For in Him we live, and move, and have our being. To say we are godlike and were made in God's image sounds foreign to some people. Using the word *like* helps us to understand the godlike concept. Like means similar, it does not mean exact. We are not God, we are just like God. We are just similar to God. We are a reflection of God. When we look in the mirror, we should see God's reflection. For instance, the moon gives off the light that illuminates the night. It is not the sun, but it is a reflection of the sun. So it is with us. Jesus is the Light of the World, and we are a reflection of that light. That is why we are called the light of the world.

Let me be clear, you are not a God but you are god-like. In other words, you are not God, but you were made in His image.

People, who are sitting around waiting for a handout, would help themselves immensely if they found out that the hand of God's power is already within them – just as God made clear to Moses at the burning bush. *God then said, 'Put your hand inside your shirt.' He slipped his hand under his shirt, then took it out. His hand had turned leprous, like snow. He said, 'Put your hand back under your shirt.' He did it, then took it back out – as healthy as before* (Exodus 4:6-7).

The Bible also declares in Acts 17:28: *For in him we live, and move, and have our being… For we are also His offspring.*

The truth is that we are defined by His divinity. Let me put it this way. We sprang up out of Him. If I may use the old expression, "We are a chip off of the old block." Let me illustrate. When my first grandchild, Channing Carlyle Benjamin, Jr., was born, they said in the delivery room that he looked just like his father. Some one else said, You have got a chip off of the old block. Both of these statements do not mean that my grandson was the exact replica of his father. Instead they meant he looked just like his dad, which makes the case that all of us as children of our Father carry His spiritual DNA match. In this instance, DNA means "Devine Name Applies." The fact is, no matter how hard we work at it, we cannot get away from the Lord. There is no hiding place on earth. The main problem we have, in accepting this truth, is we do not know who we really are in Him. It is called wrong thinking. The Bible says God's people are being *destroyed for lack of knowledge* (Hosea 4:6). We often think wrong because we are ignorant of what is right. Some would argue that this truth is relative, but my measuring stick is the Bible as the Word of God.

Of course, so much of this will be determined by what parents pass down to their children. Unfortunately, you cannot teach what you do not know, and you cannot lead where you will not go. This generation is suffering from a breakdown of the family and poor parenting. It is very difficult for children to raise children. This is the tragic residual of the epidemic of teenage pregnancy that has put the American family, in general, and the African-American family in particular, in great danger. The collapse of the family and family values is at the core of our national corruption.

I want to share a word of knowledge that can change our direction from being dependent believers to being empowered believers. It is revolutionary thinking. There is no doubt that we have got the power, but first we have to understand who God is and who we are. Do you know that if we knew who we really were, we would think differently, and as a result we would act differently? We would not do just anything and everything that comes to our minds if we knew that we were reflecting Him. We would know beyond a shadow of doubt that there are two different sides of being godlike. One side holds us accountable, and the other side makes us undefeatable and unstoppable while still holding us accountable. If we realized that we are godlike, then we would not be so mean, selfish and disobedient. We would not wear anything or look any kind of way if we knew whose image we were reflecting. As young people, we would not wear our pants halfway down our behinds because we would understand that we represented the image of God.

Unfortunately, you cannot teach what you do not know, and you cannot lead where you will not go. This generation is suffering from a breakdown of the family and poor parenting. It is very difficult for

children to raise children. This is the tragic residual of the epidemic of teenage pregnancy that has put the American family, in general, and the African-American family in particular, in great danger. The collapse of the family and family values is at the core of our national corruption.

If you had the knowledge that you are godlike, gang-banging would not be an option because that is not God's personna. You would not even think about raping somebody because you would know that God is not a sexual predator. Murder rates would go down and employment rates would go up. Hatred would be halted and jealousy would be jailed. We would not be maiming and stealing if we knew who we really were. If we knew that we carried the "I AM" inside of us, there would be more of us in college than in jail. We would see more high school drop-ins than drop outs. It has to do with right thinking because it is all in our minds.

"We can have a sound, disciplined, strong mind, and we can think the thoughts of God, reason according to the Word of God and reject the thoughts of the world," wrote Casey Treat in *Renewing the Mind*. "The lack of a sound, disciplined mind is a major problem in many people's lives today. The evidence of that lack is glaring, the failure of public schools, the number of hours the average person watches TV, the decline of real leaders and the rise of welfare cases."

Whenever we are ready to be what Jesus was to the Father, Jesus will be to us what the Father was to Him. All we have to do is step out and say, "For Christ I live and for Christ I die." Philippians 1:21 says it this way: *For to me to live is Christ, and to die is gain.* It is never too late to be great or as Spike Lee simply said, "Do the right thing." I believe that God is calling us this present generation like He called Moses out of a burning bush. Just as He spoke to him, He is speaking to us and calling us to turn our lives over completely to the One who is able to keep us from falling.

Whenever we are ready to be what Jesus was to the Father, Jesus will be to us what the Father was to Him.

We live in times of great difficulty and challenge in our world. If we were honest, many of us would have to admit that we have been dependent instead of empowered. The chaotic era, in which we live, should serve as a wake up call for those who always see God as residing on the outside. You have a lot more to offer in life when you believe that Jesus lives on the inside of you. I encourage you to invite Him in; He stands at the door and knocks. Once you allow the God of Abraham, Isaac, Jacob and Moses to live in you, then you become the power of God.

Chapter 10
Attitude Of Gratitude

'If you don't like something, change it. If you can't change it, change your attitude. Don't complain.' – Maya Angelou

Our new grandchild continued to fill our family's days with hours of joy as we soaked up the seemingly endless California sunshine in early 2008. The approaching springtime beckoned our hearts toward a new beginning once again as we happily watched the days get longer and warmer. Oh, how grateful we were to still be in the land of the living. Most of all, we were so thankful for what God is doing in our lives. The number seven in the Bible usually implies completion or the finishing of something. It is called the perfect number. The number eight usually signifies the beginning or initiation of something new. It was significant to us that little Channing Carlyle Benjamin, Jr., would be born at the end of 2007. It signaled for us the end of an era and the beginning of something new. It was like a new lease on life. It was as if we were starting all over again. Grandchildren are such a gift from God because they give you hope in the future and gratitude for the past.

If people take nothing else away from the pages of this book, I sincerely hope they understand how critical it is to think right, which in essence is the *attitude of gratitude*. The Bible says we can do nothing apart from God, but it always begins with how we think. I cannot thank author James Allen enough for planting deep in my spirit the biblical injunction in Proverbs 23:7: *as a man thinketh in his heart, so is he*. I am so grateful for this revelation, and I believe that when one fully understands it, the secret to abundant living becomes apparent. Everything begins with a thought. Our thoughts are shaped by the influences that surround us from the womb to the tomb. How our parents think, what we learn in school and the influences of the friends and associates that we gather around us are critical in the formation of right and wrong thinking. In a world of competing irrelevancies, Jesus said in John 10:10, *I am come that they might have life, and that they might have it more abundantly*. So then, it has become clear to me that we must base our thinking on the mind of Christ, which is the Word of God. What happens so often is that people want to think right without a standard. It is nearly impossible to produce right thinking apart from the truth of the Word of God. When the Bible says in Hosea 4:6 that our people are destroyed for a lack of knowledge, the *knowledge* that is referred to there is the truth of the Word of God. So then Bible study, Sunday school, church attendance and personal devotion take on a new level of significance.

So often, people ask me, "Well, how do you objectively determine whether you are thinking right or wrong?" My answer is simple. If it lines up with the mind of Christ and what Christ teaches, then it constitutes right thinking. If it does not, it will more than likely lead you to the path of wrong thinking. Our thoughts will essentially determine the quality of life that we live. If we could just master this important lesson, we could literally have heaven on earth.

Over 30 years ago, I helped introduce, to the body of Christ, the theology of "heaven on earth," which basically supported the thesis of what has been called the Lord's Prayer. In that prayer, it is stated *thy Kingdom come, thy will be done on earth as it is in heaven*. This basically means that we as believers are called to be a colony of heaven right here on earth. Heaven is not just a place we go *to* but a state of mind that we live *in*. Nobody believed in heaven more than my sainted grandmother, Marilla Roberts Jackson, but she would not allow heaven to be boxed in by traditional thinking. She believed that heaven was as much below her feet as it was above her head. She was always ahead of her time and she taught me what Jesus taught her – right thinking produces right results.

 So often, people ask me, "Well, how do you objectively determine whether you are thinking right or wrong?" My answer is simple. If it lines up with the mind of Christ and what Christ teaches, then it constitutes right thinking. If it does not, it will more than likely lead you to the path of wrong thinking.

Our thoughts will essentially determine the quality of life that we live. If we could just master this important lesson, we could literally have heaven on earth.

This theology is often confused with today's "Prosperity Gospel." When I say heaven on earth, I am not talking about money or material in and of itself. Money and materials are by-products of the way we think. Money does not produce thought: rather, thought produces money. Everything is at first spiritual before it becomes physical. The old saying goes "conceive it, believe it and achieve it." We have learned that is the short version; we must also speak it and act upon it. When we do, it manifests. Strictly speaking, it is not really about us, it is about God and what we think about God, who promised to *supply all of your need according to His riches in glory by Christ Jesus* (Philippians 4:19). What would you think if I told you that my understanding of poverty and wealth is that they are a state of mind? They have nothing to do with money. You are what you think you are. The Old Testament says in Deuteronomy 8:18, it is the Lord that gives us the power to get wealth. What I am really saying is what we think about God, who gives us wealth, has everything to do with bringing it to us or driving it away from us. The main thing is to maintain an attitude of gratitude, regardless of our circumstances. I am talking about the quality of life that we live and the privileges that God has promised us. You can have heaven on earth with or without material wealth. You can also have hell on earth with or without material wealth. These concepts have nothing to do with wealth or poverty. They have more to do with right and wrong thinking. It's all in your mind.

Over 30 years ago, I helped to introduce to the body of Christ the theology of "heaven on earth," which basically supported the thesis of what has been called the Lord's Prayer. In that prayer, it is stated *thy Kingdom come, thy will be done on earth as it is* in heaven. This basically means that we as believers are called *to* be a colony of heaven right here on earth. Heaven is not just a place we go to but a state of mind that we live *in*.

STRENGTH OUT OF WEAKNESS

The Apostle Paul put it like this in Philippians 4:4-13: *Rejoice in the Lord always: and again I say, Rejoice. Let your moderation be known unto all men. The Lord is at hand. Be careful for nothing; but in every thing by prayer and supplication with thanksgiving let your requests be made known unto God. And the peace of God, which passeth all understanding, shall keep your hearts and minds through Christ Jesus. Finally, brethren, whatsoever things are true, whatsoever things are honest, whatsoever things are just, whatsoever things are pure, whatsoever things are lovely, whatsoever things are of good report; if there be any virtue, and if there be any praise, <u>think on</u>*

these things. Those things, which ye have both learned, and received, and heard, and seen in me, do: and the God of peace shall be with you. But I rejoiced in the Lord greatly, that now at the last your care of me hath flourished again; wherein ye were also careful, but ye lacked opportunity. Not that I speak in respect of want: for I have learned, in whatsoever state I am, therewith to be content. I know both how to be abased, and I know how to abound: every where and in all things I am instructed both to be full and to be hungry, both to abound and to suffer need. I can do all things through Christ which strengtheneth me.

What Paul meant in the last verse of that passage is he recognized his strength was not his own. He was telling us that when we are weak, that is when we are strong because Christ is our strength. His words can be soothing during the times that we fall down and cannot find the strength to get back up, during times when we cannot do anything else except call on the Lord. Those are the occasions when we cannot seem to think right; the point where God steps in and replaces our thoughts with His thoughts because the joy of the Lord is our strength. Philippians 4:13 is also an answer to author Rhonda Byrne's thesis in her book _The Secret_. Although Byrne was right when she said, "What we think about is what we bring about," her book generally omits any reference to biblical material or honor to God in the traditional sense. Even though it tells some truth, it fails to sanctify _the_ Truth. As a man thinketh or _I can do all things through Christ which strengtheneth me_ was *the secret* long before her book *The Secret* was ever thought about. Byrne did not discover the truth, but she simply uncovered the truth in a new way to a new age, and sold millions of books in the process. The real secret is that Jesus Christ has the power to change the way we think.

It is no secret that we sometimes give our children too much, too fast, when it is our love that they need the most. In the latest movie version of Lorraine Hansberry's classic Broadway play *A Raisin in the Sun*, which was recently broadcast on ABC, Walter Lee Younger Jr. (Sean "P. Diddy" Combs), taught his 12-year-old son, Travis Younger (Justin Martin), that dignity, integrity and respect are worth far more than money – even enough money to buy a new house in the suburbs.

The real secret is that Jesus Christ has the power to change the way we think.

When Paul wrote in Philippians 4:4 that we should rejoice in the Lord always, his point was that our adverse circumstance may be our *present reality,* but it is not our *future promise*. To understand this principle, we must first learn to think right. Philippians 4:5 says *let your moderation be known to all men. The Lord is at hand.* We have to learn how to be moderate in dress, behavior and habit. When we think this way, we are careful not to overdress, under dress, overeat, eat too little or overspend. Philippians

4:6 also urges us to *be careful for nothing; but in every thing by prayer and supplication with thanksgiving let your requests be made known unto God.* This verse explicitly instructs us on how we are to petition God for help. Too many times we go to God complaining and whining. Instead if we make our requests known to Him with thanksgiving it will make a tremendous difference in how God responds. Additionally, when we petition the Lord through a humble, sincere and grateful spirit, *the peace of God, which passeth all understanding, shall keep our hearts and minds through Christ Jesus* (Philippians 4:7). No matter what comes our way, we can rejoice in knowing that we carry with us the peace of God. *Finally brethren whatsoever things are true, whatsoever things are honest, whatsoever things are just, whatsoever things are pure, whatsoever things are lovely, whatsoever things are good and of good report; think on these things. Those things which ye have both learned, received, and heard and seen in me do and the God of peace shall be with you* (Philippians 4:8-9). If we replace all of our *stinking thinking* with thoughts of truth, joy, purity, honesty and justice, we will enjoy an incredible peace.

It is no secret that we sometimes give our children too much, too fast, when it is our love that they need the most... Dignity, integrity and respect are worth far more than money – even enough money to buy a new house in the suburbs.

CIRCUMSTANCE IS A SMOKESCREEN

Many people are depressed by the circumstances in which they find themselves. But we should never allow ourselves to become prisoners of our present circumstances because they really have nothing to do with our future promises. Circumstance is a smokescreen. The Bible has a word for us about circumstances: as the old saying goes, "This too shall pass." If we think right, we will not put ourselves in a position of captivity but of conquest. This can be accomplished by thinking liberation not incarceration, joy instead of sadness, love in place of hate, and gratitude not ingratitude. In other words, we will exude an attitude of gratitude. When we pray, we should express this same gratitude. We should develop the practice of being grateful and gracious to people, realizing that no one has to do anything for us. As a matter of fact, thankfulness ought to pour out of us. It should be a character trait that is spontaneous and unconditional because the attitude of gratitude is a part of the law of attraction. It is a part of the magnetic force that we constantly send out. What we send out is what we will receive in return.

God is love. Love is the most powerful thing in the world but gratitude is right behind it. As I have said throughout this book, what we think about is what we will bring about. Taking this a step further, what we think about and are *thankful* about will come about. I want only the best for the millions of precious people that God allows me to minister to every week over the radio, television, Internet and from the pulpit. I want them to enjoy all the health, wealth, and happiness that they have always wanted. And I sincerely believe that if we change our way of thinking, we will not be able to stop those blessings from coming to us. The Bible speaks about blessings literally overcoming, overwhelming, and running after us, if we listen to the voice of the Lord (Deuteronomy 28:2).

We need to keep in mind where the real battle is occurring for control of our lives: the mind. For example, many people are constantly grappling with how to take off weight and keep it off. I tell them first and foremost that food is not our enemy. We have not become overweight because of food. Our problem is our thoughts about food. The same principle applies when it comes to our thinking about money. This is really critical for us to understand. Money is not our enemy. We sometimes hear people who attend church say things like, "I don't see why they have to have all that money" or "All they talk about is money." But if we could just get over all of the busy talk about giving money to the work of the Lord, the money that we give would come back to us multiplied many times over. God did not say money was evil, He said *the love of money is the root of all evil* (1 Timothy 6:10). The two statements mean different things. If we start sowing money and not worrying about how much we are giving, we will receive far in excess of what we sowed into God's work. If we do not focus on how much we weigh, but what weight we want to be, we will get some incredible results.

> **God is love. Love is the most powerful thing in the world but gratitude is right behind it.**

An attitude of gratitude is attraction power, while in-gratitude works just the opposite. Ungrateful attitudes repel and reject everything and anything with which we come in contact. We have to be thankful for everything God gives us. When we thank God for something, we are replacing a negative thought with a positive thought. Conversely, when we focus on being poor or overweight or lonely all the time, we are attracting poverty, obesity and loneliness directly to us. We have to be clear about what we want from God. When we ask God for something, we must believe that He will grant our request and be open to receive it. A lot of our problem is we pray for something, get it and do not know what to do with it. This is a negative manifestation that was based on wrong thinking. The reason we are in debt is because we think about debt all the time. Right thinking would have us instead pondering wealth, and our bills being paid. It would have us being thankful for what we have instead of moping over what we do not have.

The book of Deuteronomy says how dare we go before God and not be grateful. Deuteronomy 32:6 talks specifically about being grateful: *Don't you realize it is God you are treating like this? This is crazy; don't you have any sense of reverence? Isn't this your father who created you, who made you and gave you a place on earth?* After all, God has done everything for us, given everything to us, and made us everything we are. How can we not be grateful to Him? If we do not pay attention, we will take things from people without saying "Thank you." In fact, we are raising a generation of children who have not been taught the importance of saying "Thank you." We need to teach our children and grandchildren how to thank people, which sometimes only requires writing a simple note or making a quick phone call. When we thank somebody immediately and voluntarily, it opens the door for us to receive many more blessings. That is why I encourage people not to base the rearing of their children on what western civilization has taught us, but search the scriptures to find out the mind of Christ on parenting. Western civilization has taught us how to raise money, but it has not taught us how to raise children. We have put technology in our children's hands, but no theology in their heads and hearts.

My grandmother worked me over real good on ingratitude. When she was upset with me, she would say that I was an "ingrate," which means that I was ungrateful to her and for what she had done for me. When she referred to me as ingrate, it was like cutting me with a knife, and she knew it, too. This happened most often when I was thinking about gratitude but failing to speak it or act it.

What we think, we have to speak and ultimately act. No person in his or her right mind wants to be an ingrate. I always felt extremely grateful to her for rescuing me, raising me, and basically giving me everything by the grace of God.

There would be far less friction in our marriages, relationships, and among our co-workers if we were walking expressions of gratitude. As a famous cartoonist once wrote, "We have seen the enemy and he is us." If we can change our thoughts, we will change our lives. Gratitude is an attitude. When we begin talking about what we do not have, we open the door to participating in negativity. Many of us are focusing too much on what we do not have instead of thanking God for what we do have and asking Him for what we need. Instead of dwelling on what we do not have, we ought to flip the script and say *I can do all things through Christ who strengthens me.* Or "I can do anything that the will of God has for me. Nothing shall be impossible to me!"

When we thank somebody immediately and voluntarily, it opens the door for us to receive many more blessings. That is why I encourage people not to base the rearing of children on what western civilization has taught us, but search the scriptures to find out the mind of Christ on parenting. Western civilization has taught us how to raise money, but it has not taught us how to raise children. We have put

technology in their hands, but no theology in their heads and hearts.

Far too many of us are short circuiting our attraction power when we, for instance, are grateful to our bosses for our jobs but never tell them so. Or we appreciate our husbands or our wives and children yet never express that gratitude to them. This is an important principle of the law of attraction. We cannot just think it and expect to be blessed – we have to speak it and act on what we say.

Many people have brought favor on my life but I had to first think I wanted to meet them. A perfect example is Howard Thurman, who was 40 years older than me. I never knew anything about him when I first heard of his reputation. He was Dean of the Boston University Chapel, and Dr. Martin Luther King's mentor and all of that, but I decided one day that I had to get to know this great man. Even though Thurman lived in San Francisco at the time, God brought him to Indianapolis one day, and since then great favor has come upon me because of the relationship we developed. It is still a blessing to me to this day. Many of us are deceiving ourselves because we are thinking what we want, but are short circuiting the power to make it happen by not saying it and acting upon it.

We are raising a generation of children who have not been taught the importance of saying "thank you."

THE RIGHT FOCUS

We cannot rush God in the blessing process. When we begin to operate with right thinking, hour by hour and day by day, we will start to prosper. The things that were holding us back will not be able to do so anymore. We have to start thinking the results we desire and speaking them. We should be grateful for what we have because we could have nothing. Though we have all experienced problems, pitfalls and pains, none of us has been crucified the way Jesus was crucified. As bad off as we think we are, there is always somebody worse off. At least most of us who live in the developed countries have enough to eat, clothes to wear and a roof over our heads. Because whatever we focus on gravitates toward us, it is important to think about what we want, and be thankful for what we already have.

Sometimes it is difficult for us to think right, mainly because we are fighting a battle with the media over who will influence our minds. The inexhaustible information age is contaminating all of us. Unless we find ways to counteract the voluminous information that comes at us from 200 different directions through the media, with *whatever things are lovely, true or of good report,* we are actually going to speak about that which we hear the most. If we are not careful and conscientious about what is entering our minds, we are going to receive everything that the media advertises. Deliverance comes when we stop thinking about what we want and start thanking God for what we have. For instance, we may drive a compact car but really need a larger sedan. In this case, we should be grateful for the compact car because if we are not, it will block our chance to get the sedan. God wants to know whether He can trust us with what He has given us before He is comfortable with giving us more. In other words, if we learn to be content with the compact, the Lord will know for sure that we can handle the full-size model. If God cannot trust us with the $100 that He gives us each week to pay our tithes faithfully – not sporadically – He is not going to be inclined to increase our income. If the Lord cannot trust us for the $100, He surely is not going to entrust us with the $1,000 or $1 million. We cannot walk into that kind of wealth, unless we have integrity. Too many times, we have allowed the enemy to deceive us with the lie that it is not important how we disburse our money. Falling for this deception guarantees that we will be stuck in financial bondage. Make no mistake about it that money is as important to God as it is to us. It is a gift that the Lord has designed to bless people. The more we give, the more He will give us. Some poor people remain poor because they cannot be trusted, even with the meager resources they already have. They want to get more but do not want to give more. They want to grow but do not want to sow.

Deliverance comes when we stop thinking about what we want and start thanking God for what we have.

Someone once said many people, who live their lives rightly, are kept in poverty in all other ways by their lack of gratitude. It is possible to be saved, sanctified, filled with the Holy Ghost and speaking in tongues, and still be poorer than *Job's turkey*. The difference between folks who are barely getting by and the people they admire is the way they think. People who have the wealth that other people want, do not run money away from them; money knows their address. They do not push people away from them; people want to be around them. Why on earth would anyone want to be in the company of somebody who is spiteful? Hatefulness, ungratefulness, selfishness, and self-centeredness go together. The people who espouse those characteristics really do not know God. When we are jealous of people, it does not do anything but put us in spiritual jail and prohibit our blessings from reaching us. Again, what we think about we bring about. Negative thinking brings negative results and vice versa. In addition, what we call right thinking does not make sense to some people. In 1 Corinthians 3:19, the Apostle Paul says, *What the world calls smart, God calls stupid. It's written in Scripture, He exposes the chicanery of the chic.* We need to put our thoughts on what we *do* have, and block out thoughts about what we *do not* have. Wrong thinking is going to produce wrong results every single time. Instead, we should make a list of what we are grateful for. The list that we come up with will far outweigh what we would have complained about in the first place.

Exercising gratitude will attract grace and blessings to us in the long run. Instead of saying, "TGIF (Thank God it's Friday)," we should say TGIM (Thank God it's Monday), and be grateful that we have been allowed to live to see the beginning of a brand new week. We should be thinking with gratitude about what is ahead of us not behind us. It is time to break the habit of looking into the rear view mirror. In fact, we need to thank God for the privilege of seeing a new day each and every day.

We need to put our thoughts on what we *do* have, and block out thoughts about what we *do not* have. Wrong thinking is going to produce wrong results every single time. Instead, we should make a list of what we are grateful for. The list that we come up with will far outweigh what we would have complained about in the first place... We should be thinking with gratitude about what is ahead of us not behind us. It is time to break the habit of looking into the rear view mirror. In fact, we need to thank God for the privilege of seeing a new day each and every day.

As we think, so are we. What we can see in our minds is already in our hands. It is a seed that we will sow if we are to grow. If our minds are a pearl, we can do anything in the world. What we think about, and are thankful for, we will surely bring about. It is called right thinking, and it all begins in our minds.

Chapter 11
His Eye Is On The Sparrow

'I sing because I'm happy. I sing because I'm free. His eye is on the sparrow, and I know He watches me.' – Civilla Martin and Charles Gabriel

Kyson Stowell does not realize it yet, but he is a miracle baby. The infant miraculously survived the tornadoes that smashed the Tennessee town of Castilian Springs on the evening of February 5, 2008. When a tornado swept through the area, 11-month-old Kyson was hurled into a field about 100 yards from where his home once stood. He was found lying face down in the mud by two firefighters about 1:30 a.m. the following morning. Rescuers first thought the baby, who was covered over with grass and mud, was a toy doll. The field where they found him was strewn with debris, including a couch from somebody's home, an entire car engine and transmission, and bricks from a nearby post office that had been leveled by the powerful storm. The infant had been overlooked by another search crew that had hunted through the field earlier that night. Kyson's mother, Kerri Stowell, 24, was not as fortunate. Her body was found later in the same field. Investigators indicated that the child would not have survived the cold night if not found when he was. The twisters killed at least 59 people in Tennessee, Kentucky, Mississippi, Alabama and Arkansas. This miraculous story is a reminder that God constantly watches over every person in the world. There is a tremendous need in the body of Christ to understand that God really loves us and has not forgotten us.

We are living in very difficult times. Terrible things are happening around us, both in our natural environment and in our families. Often, it seems that we live in an age of agitation and an era of edginess. Everyone is on edge, from the privileged to the poor. People have gotten to be so uptight that we can hardly say anything to anybody anymore without them becoming offended. Today preachers are using profanity in the pulpit. There is too much of the world in the church, and not enough church in the world. There are wars and rumors of war but we are not to panic; rather, we are to persevere. What we are going through was predicted in the book of Matthew 24:6, which tells us: *When reports come in of wars and rumored wars, keep your head and don't panic. This is routine history; this is no sign of the end.*

There is too much of the world in the church and not enough church in the world.

Speaking of wars, we are currently fighting one in Iraq that we cannot win because we have followed a foreign policy that makes no sense and has been built on lies and deception. And although we have made tremendous progress on social issues in our country, there is still evidence all over the nation of the terrible beast called racism, which is causing people to still have to march in the streets – even 40 years after the death of Dr. Martin Luther King Jr. – to secure rights that they should have received a long time ago. The Jena Six case is just one sad example of the day-by-day frustration of being born Black in America. But in spite of the problems that we are struggling with in these turbulent times, we must remember that God has promised to never leave us nor forsake us. He will never abandon us, no matter how insignificant we think that we are to Him. Listen to what Jesus says about this in Matthew 10:28-33: *Don't be bluffed into silence by the threats of bullies. There's nothing they can do to your soul, your core being. Save your fear for God, who holds your entire life – body and soul – in His hands. What's the price of a pet canary? Some loose change, right? And God cares what happens to it even more than you do. He pays even greater attention to you, down to the last detail – even numbering the hairs on your head! So don't be intimidated by all this bully talk. You're worth more than a million canaries. Stand up for Me against world opinion and I'll stand up for you before my Father in heaven. If you turn tail and run, do you think I'll cover for you?* This may appear hard to believe, but God's eye is even on the sparrow. If the Lord makes it His business to keep track of a little bird, then surely God is concerned about everything that happens in our lives.

In spite of all of the many personal challenges that we are dealing with, we can overcome them if we think right. For instance, we can succeed in making our marriages work, we can succeed in keeping our families from disintegrating, we can succeed in meeting our financial obligations, we can succeed in paying our covenants, tithes, offerings and pledges, and we can succeed in helping our children with their problems if we live by the Word of God as expressed and experienced in the Holy Bible.

I want you to know something about God. It is really not so much that the enemy is trying to wreck our marriages and take our money. It is not so much that the devil is trying to take something away from us, as it is that he wants more than anything else to cut off and chip away at our confidence in the wisdom, care, and guidance that the Lord wants to provide for us – if only we would think right. In other words, the enemy knows full well that if he can get at our minds, he can get at our marriages. If he can get at our marriages, he can get at our families. And if he can get to our families, he can destroy the nation.

What I have been trying to say in these pages is that we need to stand fast and strong on our faith. We need to resolve that come what may, whatever is going on around us, there is a God who has His eye on us. No matter what is happening in world events or our individual lives, God is not distracted from meeting our needs. He loves us so much that He gave Jesus, His only begotten Son, to die for us way back on Calvary. Part of the reason that I wrote this book is because I wanted to remind people that they must hold on and hold out, for help is on the way. We must keep our confidence in God and the fact that He cares. If His eye is on the little sparrow, it is certain that He is concerned about us.

It is not so much that the devil is trying to take something away from us, as it is that he wants more than anything else to cut off and chip away at our confidence in the wisdom, care, and guidance that God wants to provide for us – if only we would think right. In other words, the enemy knows full well that if he can get at our minds, he can get at our marriages. If he can get at our marriages, he can get at our families. And if he can get to our families, he can destroy the nation.

I appeal to you. Do not become discouraged when you are traveling through one of life's valleys. Just because you are going through something, does not mean that God is not walking with you. I am reminded about the story of the "Footprints in the Sand." It is an account of a man having a dream one night, in which he is walking on a beach with the Lord. As would be expected, they leave two sets of footprints in the sand behind them. The tracks are supposed to represent various stages of the man's life. When he looks back at the tracks, he sees that at some points, the two trails dwindle to one, especially at the lowest and most discouraging moments of his life. He questions the Lord, believing that God must have abandoned him during those times. But the Lord said in response, "During your times of trial and suffering, when you see only one set of footprints, it was then that I carried you." Thank God that we have all had those times, when there have been only one set of footprints behind us.

As the Bible declares in Matthew 10, God personalizes His relationship with each one of us. Every person on earth is important to Him. Our journeys are important; what we are going through is important; our maturation and aging are important; our high blood pressure and diabetes are important. The problems that we are going through with our children are important because every hair on our heads is numbered by God! In other words, He knows everything about what we are going through and when we reach our most difficult days, He will pick us up and carry us. We can find solace in the truth that we do not have to do this thing alone. It is so good to know that at 3 o'clock in the morning, we do not have to wake up all by ourselves. Not only can God keep an accurate count of our hair strands because He is God all by Himself, but He is better than that – He is our Father. We dare not think for half a second that our Father does not care about His sons or daughters. Whether you are flying on an airplane, riding in your car, or just looking in the mirror, you can be assured that He cares. We are worth more than a million sparrows to Jesus. God knows our names, addresses and telephone numbers by heart – all of them. The Lord is also aware that the enemy tries to make us think that God is more interested in world events than in us. On the contrary, God knows who caused the current state of world affairs – man did. God did not start the wars in Iraq and Afghanistan. He did not hang nooses in Jena, Louisiana; that is our doing. But through it all, God's eye has never left us. I am reminded of an old hymn we used to sing: *He walks with me and He talks with me and He tells me I'm His own. The joy we share as we tarry there none other has ever known!*

Knowing that God is close to us and has His eye on us will give us confidence when we fly on an airplane. It will reassure us when trouble is all around us. God is that close – as close as our breathing. In other words, He knows our conditions, positions, personalities, DNA, chemistry, and thought patterns. Whatever we are dealing with, the Lord knows all about it. He is there as a strong tower and a walking stick. Proverbs 18:10 says: *God's name is a place of protection – good people can run there and be safe.* God personalizes His relationships and recognizes our condition. It is incredible that although there are millions of animal species in the world, when just one sparrow falls to the ground, God is aware of it. That is a pretty deep thought to consider. Because of the finite way in which we think, it is hard for us to understand how someone could know everyone and everything that He created on a personal basis. The only way to grasp this concept is we must accept the fact that the Lord truly is God and is concerned about everything that affects our lives, even something as inconsequential as a hangnail. The Lord loves everything He created and all that God created is good. He is especially concerned about our health. We should remember this the next time we go to the doctor and the physician tries to tell us that we are old, worn out, and only have a few more days in this life. We need to remember right then that the One who created us, the One who saw us through our teenage years, the One who allowed us to have our children and rear our families, the same One who brought us this far by faith, has not brought us all this way to leave us now. If we really believe the Bible, we will have none of it. The Bible says we will live and not die. Psalm 118:17 declares: *I shall not die, but live, and declare the works of the Lord.* This is our time to live, and no time to even think about giving up. Even though I am older than I have ever been, I have never felt better in my life than I do today. In fact, I have never been more confident, focused, and determined because the glory of the Lord is upon my house and upon my life. I am not going to quit, nor give up over some ache or pain. God knows all about my aches, and He will see me through every one of my pains. This is why the Bible says, *Yea, though I walk through the valley of the shadow of death, I will fear no evil: for Thou art with me; Thy rod and thy staff they comfort me* (Psalm 23:4).

The interesting thing about Matthew 10:29 is in the original language, it was not so much a bird falling from a tree that David was talking about, it was really more of the broken-wing syndrome. It could be something physical, spiritual, or psychological that gets broken in our lives. Have you ever seen a broken-wing bird? Even though it falls to the ground, God knows what it is going through and He sees exactly where it lands. Remember the story of Jacob wrestling all night with an angel (Genesis 32:22-29)? *And he rose up that night, and took his two wives, and his two womenservants, and his eleven sons, and passed over the ford Jabbok. And he took them, and sent them over the brook, and sent over that he had. And Jacob was left alone; and there wrestled a man with him until the breaking of the day. And when he saw that he prevailed not against him, he touched the hollow of his thigh; and the hollow of Jacob's thigh was out of joint, as he wrestled with him. And he said, Let me go, for the day breaketh. And he said, I will not let thee go, except thou bless me. And he said unto him, What is thy name? And he said, Jacob. And he said, Thy name shall be called no more Jacob, but Israel: for as a prince hast thou power with God and with men, and hast prevailed. And Jacob asked him, and said, Tell me, I pray thee, thy name. And he said, Wherefore is it that thou dost ask after my name? And he blessed him there.*

Just as the Lord knew what caused Jacob to walk with a limp, He knows all about our limps. The fact is that God might have even made our "limps" possible, so we can get closer to Him. He may have allowed us to experience dysfunctions and discomforts in life, so that we would have to lean on Him as our walking sticks. It could be that the Lord allowed us to limp a little, so that we would know, beyond a shadow of doubt, He still cares for us. Every little bout with high blood pressure, diabetes, and arthritis is just a reminder that when we are limping, we have to depend on God. Actually, every little problem we face reminds us that when we are weak, that is when God is strong. Friends, you can depend on God. We cannot depend on ourselves to straighten our limbs.

Pastor Joel Osteen has said, "You may make some mistakes but that doesn't make you a sinner. You've got the very nature of God on the inside of you." In other words, mistakes do not make a sinner but disobedience does. All we have to do is read the story of Jacob, the deceiver, to know that disobeying or running away from God will only result in making us lame. Instead we have to depend on Him for everything we need and do. It all begins in our minds. When our minds are renewed, we realize that what was impossible is *really* possible. God personalizes and recognizes the broken wings in our lives. He specializes in the things that are impossible. And He sees the limps coming long before we ever start wrestling with the angels. I love that old hymn: *Have you any rivers that you think are uncrossable? Have you any mountains that you cannot tunnel through? God specializes in things that are impossible. He will make a way for you.*

This is our time to live and no time to even think about giving up. Even though I am older than I have ever been, I have never felt better in my life than I do today. In fact, I have never been more confident, focused, and determined because the glory of the Lord is upon my house and upon my life. I am not going to quit, or give up over some ache or a pain. God knows all about my aches and He will see me through every one of my pains. This is why the Bible says, *Yea, though I walk through the valley of the shadow of death, I will fear no evil: for thou art with me; thy rod and thy staff they comfort me (Psalm 23:4).*

Has the Lord ever made a way for you? Sometimes I forget how many times that God has wondrously made a way for me. And if He did it in the past, He will surely do it again. Why wouldn't God do that? Do not forget that He is keenly aware of every minute detail about us. Though we stumble and fall and whatever kind of drama is going on in our lives, whether it relates to joblessness, illness, or business, God still loves us and cares about us. Although God cares about the sparrow, He cares about us even more. Whatever is going on in our lives, we have to put it all in His hands. The value of anything is determined by whose hands it is in. I decided, a long time ago, to put it all in His hands, which makes things so much easier. Grass does not have to strain to grow, and rivers do not have to bend to flow because they have been in the Lord's hands since the beginning.

It could be that the Lord allowed us to limp a little, so that we would know beyond a shadow of doubt that He still cares for us. Every little bout with high blood pressure, diabetes, and arthritis is just a reminder that when we are limping, we have to depend on God. Actually, every little problem we face reminds us that when we are weak that is when God is strong. Friends, you can depend on God.

Here is a further illustration of that point. A baseball bat in my hands is worth about $30, but in Barry Bond's hands it is worth $30 million. A basketball in my hands is worth approximately $35, but in Kobe Bryant's hands $35 million. A football in my hands is worth roughly $40, but in Peyton Manning's hands $40 million. A golf club in my hands might get you hit, but the same golf club in Tiger Wood's hands can bring him a cool $100 million. A nail that pierces my hand might send me to the hospital, but the nails that were driven into Jesus' hands will save our souls, make us whole, heal our bodies, regulate our minds and set us free.

A nail that pierces my hand might send me to the hospital, but the nails that were driven into Jesus' hands will save our souls, make us whole, heal our bodies, regulate our minds and set us free.

God's eye is on the sparrow and I know He watches us. It does not matter that we are going through some stuff His eye is still on us. There might be some trouble in our way, but the Lord continues to keep us in His sight. Food and gas prices may be up and income may be down, but God is good and God is good all the time. God knows and He cares. When we are having a hard time making ends meet, He has got His eye directly on us. During such times, I think of the old hymn: *Why should I feel discouraged whenever the shadows begin to fall? Why should my heart be weary and long for heaven and home? With Jesus as my portion, constant friend is He. His eye is on that sparrow and I know He watches me. I sing because I'm happy. I sing because I'm free. His eye is on the sparrow, and I know He watches me...*

Chapter 12
On Your Mark, Get Set, Go...

'In golf as in life it is the follow through that makes the difference.' – Alicia Keys

The sociologists tell us that a child's character is shaped very early in life. An African proverb declares: "As the twig is bent, so grows the tree." What parents and other adults do to impact and influence the minds of children has a profound effect on the quality of life in our country, and predicts the kinds of problems that our leaders will have to face later on. This is one of the reasons that I started a pre-school program called Respect Academy in the early 1990s. The school's curriculum emphasizes teaching children self-respect, respect for others, cultural awareness, courtesy, kindness, self-esteem and discipline.

If my beloved grandmother, Marilla Roberts Jackson, who took me in when I was only *knee high to a grasshopper*, was alive today she would say the disrespect that we see being expressed by young people all over the world is rooted in how children have been mistreated, miseducated, misdirected and unloved as infants and toddlers. She would say the blame should not be put on the children for the way they are behaving. But instead, grown ups should look into their own hearts, homes and churches, where children have been devalued and segregated as second-class citizens and kept at arms length from the life of the church and community. Mama was right, of course. All people are profoundly affected by the adults that they come into contact with when they are children. We must never underestimate the impact that we have upon the mental sky of children in the first three years of their life. Some educators and psychologists have said that in the first 36 months of a child's life, character and conduct is formed.

"During the first three years of a person's life, their languages are learned, their personality is formed, and their sexuality is established," said Thurman Gordon, a retired teacher and member of our congregation. It is generally accepted that the first three years of a child's life are the most important developmental years with life lasting effects.

I make a practice of asking people who attend services at Light of the World to shake hands and talk to the folks sitting next to them. I do this, primarily, because I strongly believe that love must be translated into *action*. There are two main reasons that I want folks to interact at church. First, it would be bad manners to let them sit through a service two hours long without giving them an opportunity to greet their neighbors, at the very least. Second, the Apostle James tells us that faith without works is dead: *Dear friends, do you think you'll get anywhere in this if you learn all the right words but never do anything?*

Does merely talking about faith indicate that a person really has it? For instance, you come upon an old friend dressed in rags and half-starved and say, 'Good morning, friend! Be clothed in Christ! Be filled with the Holy Spirit!' and walk off without providing so much as a coat or a cup of soup – where does that get you? Isn't it obvious that God-talk without God-acts is outrageous nonsense? (James 2:14-17). And in the same sense, isn't it strange for human beings to sit next to each other or walk past each other and never smile or greet? Everything that I ever learned about life teaches me that human beings are designed to love one another – not just in words, but in actions. How can you say that you love God and never speak to or smile at your neighbor? This is what I call Good Samaritan 101. We can never graduate to a deep expression of love, if we cannot acquire the bare basics of human interaction. People no longer want to just hear about Jesus; they want to see Him in you and me.

By the same token, it is impossible to show love without action. The more than familiar hit song "What The World Needs Now Is Love" became so popular it was recorded by a host of singers. Written and composed by Hal David and Burt Bacharach, the soul-stirring tune has struck a chord with a generation of people all over the world. Luther Van Dross' immortal ballad "Power of Love" is just another example of lyrics that speak to the power of the love emotion. Both of these songs move beyond feelings and call us to action. Can you imagine an Olympic trial of the 100-meter dash and the starter shouting only, "On your mark, get set…" but then saying nothing else? The key word is "go," which actually starts the race. All the rest is preparation. Love is an action verb. That being the case, in order for us to love someone through action, we must first think right. Some of the dysfunctions in our nation, including poverty, homelessness, drugs, violence, broken homes and divorce, just to name a few, are only symptoms of an underlying cause. The true cause of this chaos begins with the way people think. Again, it's all in your mind.

People no longer want to just hear about Jesus; they want to see Him in you and me.

In her devotional book *Battlefield of the Mind*, evangelist Joyce Meyer declared that the enemy works slowly, but diligently and in small ways to distort our thinking. "Rarely does he approach us through direct assault or frontal attacks," Meyer noted. "All Satan needs is an opening – and opportunity to inject unholy, self-centered thoughts into our heads. If we don't kick them out, they stay inside. And he can continue his evil, destructive plan."

Right thinking and right loving are based on a faith foundation. A foundation of faith must be built upon the Word of God, which teaches us that everything works by love. Yet we know that even love is produced by right thinking. Even our ability to love properly comes from right thinking. When the enemy comes to hassle our home, rattle our relationships and sidetrack our spirituality, we must be able to stand on a strong foundation. One of the most effective ways to overcome the enemy's assault is to respond by using the sword of the spirit, which is the Word of God, against any and every attack the enemy makes. Jesus used this same strategy, with phenomenal results, whenever Satan tried to attack Him. We can see this illustrated in the Gospels, when Jesus had just come out of the wilderness and Satan approached Him with trick challenges and questions. Jesus answered each one of them with the preface. For example, God said in Matthew 18:18 that we must speak with the authority of a believer, just as Jesus did: *Verily I say unto you, Whatsoever ye shall bind on earth shall be bound in heaven: and whatsoever ye shall loose on earth shall be loosed in heaven.* It also demands that we have an intimate knowledge about what Jesus said and did, so we can walk in His footsteps.

Some of the dysfunction in our nation, including poverty, homelessness, drugs, violence, broken homes and divorce, just to name a few, are only symptoms of an underlying cause. The true cause of this chaos begins with the way people think. Again, it's all in your mind.

Dr. Howard Thurman, the late great Dean of the Chapel at Boston University, used to say to me, "Tom, in every man there is an inward sea, and on that sea there is an island, and on that island there is an altar, and on that altar there is an angel with a flaming sword, and nothing absolutely nothing crosses that altar without your inward authority or inward consent."

ALL IN THE FAMILY

The main reason that people have such difficulty showing love on a consistent basis is because the flesh is first and foremost concerned about "me, myself and I." This is at its source an ego problem. The only way to combat the natural pulling of the flesh is to put the ego in the backseat of the car and strap it in a seatbelt. Too often, the flesh has us thinking something like this: "Well, I know that the right thing to do is to forgive her, but I just cannot forget what she did to me; it hurt me too bad." This kind of thinking usually means our enmity is out of control and our personal relationships are a mess. I have seen this too many times in my lifetime. Brothers and sisters have not spoken to each other for years, parents have not laid eyes on their children since Lord only knows when, and we wonder why young people think so little of others – and most of all themselves.

We cannot operate in the flesh and the Spirit at the same time. When we decline to engage a neighbor or a passerby with a polite greeting, despite the fact that the Holy Spirit is encouraging us to do so, especially when among Christians, we run the risk of missing a blessing that God has earmarked specifically for us. If we can get above the pettiness of the flesh and begin to flow in love with action, it will work wonders for us. When we are truly flowing in God's love, we will be quick to give up our seat when somebody else enters a crowded room, swift to apologize when we are clearly wrong, and just as fast to forgive when others have done wrong to us.

'In every man there is an inward sea, and on that sea there is an island, and on that island there is an altar, and on that altar there is an angel with a flaming sword, and nothing absolutely nothing crosses that altar without your inward authority or inward consent.' – Howard Thurman, African-American theologian and prolific author.

The truth is that our families also include our brothers and sisters in Christ. When we gather together for church, bible study, rehearsal, or to feed the poor, it is like a family reunion. Jesus made this point as He was teaching in the synagogue one day, when His mother and brother showed up outside and asked to speak with Him. *Jesus didn't respond directly, but said, 'Who do you think My mother and brothers are?' He then stretched out His hand toward His disciples. 'Look closely. These are My mother and brothers. Obedience is thicker than blood. The person who obeys My heavenly Father's will is My brother and sister and mother'* (Matthew 12:48-50).

One of the main reasons that a couple stays married for many years is because one of them has learned to love the other one no matter what they go through. It is called unconditional love. It is also called agape. Some people still enjoy regular contact with their children because they have learned to love them this way. What I mean is the right thing to do is to continue loving our children, even through the rebellious stages that almost all of them will go through. Sometimes tough love can be misunderstood as lacking sensitivity and tenderness. We love our children in many different ways, but the bottom line is to *love them to life*. Love has resurrection power. We never give up on our children, even though we sometimes have to love them from a distance. More often than not, a parent's expression of pure love and sometimes tough love toward a wayward child is what causes that child to turn his life around. A great example of this is the biblical story of the prodigal son. When the son was carelessly wasting away his life, stuck in the muck and mire of the pig pen, what did the father do? Did he besmirch his son's character to everyone he encountered? Did he send his servants to beat up and ridicule his disobedient son? Did he curse his boy's memory and disavow him? Did he send a SWAT team to extricate his son from the mess that he was in? No, the father was not inclined to do that. Instead, he waited patiently for the son, who he had trained up in the way he should go. And sure enough, one day he looked down the road and saw his son coming back home. He was returning home humble, broken, emotionally spent, and regretful for his time of riotous living. His father welcomed him back with open arms. As a matter of fact, he ordered that his son be clothed in fine apparel, put a ring on his finger and held a banquet in honor of his return. That is exactly the way the people of God need to learn how to love. Mahatma Gandhi said, "Forgiveness is not an act of weakness, it is one of the highest forms of love. The weak can never forgive. Forgiveness is the attribute of the strong."

Some of us have been handicapped by our thought process, by our inability to love even those who hate us, as hard as that is to do. Whether or not we want to admit it, unforgiveness is at the very core of our unhappiness. If that is the case for you, let it go. Forget that mean-spirited remark that was made about you by someone else. Sure it was upsetting, but you can begin to turn the tables by chipping away at it. If we are going to be like Jesus, it will first require that we take a good, hard look at the cross. Some people go through divorces, which are painful enough, still hating the person that they have already detached themselves from. I won't tell you that the chipping process is going to be easy or accomplished without you experiencing hurt. You are not likely to get through it without suffering some pain, but God can absorb the pain for you. The healing process has to begin with the mind – the way we think. Because after all, isn't it all in our minds?

'Forgiveness is not an act of weakness, it is one of the highest forms of love. The weak can never forgive. Forgiveness is the attribute of the strong.' – Mahatma Gandhi, renowned Indian peace activist and spiritual leader.

Some churches sing the song "They'll Know We Are Christians By Our Love." Oh, really – will they? The fact is that people won't be able to tell we are Christians by how soulful we can sing, how profound we can preach or how crowded is our congregation. I could not have survived all these years in ministry in my town, if I had not learned to love my enemies and followed that love up with action. If I had not learned to love, I would have been a casualty of the self-hate of others, which is also known as the green monster, in our community, called jealousy. We now have coined the phrase "haterism." Its object is to kill another person with unkind words and deeds. Interestingly enough, I have often said the haters, in my life, have really helped me to achieve, sometimes more than the ones who have smiled in my face but harbored hate in their hearts.

When people do us wrong, it is not something we should take personally. The late Rev. Clarence Cobb, affection-ately known as "Preacher," who served the least, the last and the lost of Chicago's southside, often told his First Church of Deliverance congregation, and even his wider radio audience, "It does not matter what you think of me, it only matters what I think of you. I will not get to heaven based on what you think of me. I will only get to heaven based on what I think of you." Any form of hatred, jealousy or enmity toward another person is wrong thinking. It follows that when we are thinking wrong, we become distracted and lose our power. At that point, we are in danger of sliding into an impoverished spirit. Kenneth B. Clark put it this way: "We can destroy ourselves by cynicism and disillusion just as effectively as by bombs."

'It does not matter what you think of me, it only matters what I think of you. I will not get to heaven based on what you think of me. I will only get to heaven based on what I think of you.' – Rev. Clarence H. Cobb, African-American minister and social activist.

Rhonda Byrne, author of *The Secret*, said, "If you go back over your life and focus on the difficulties from the past, you are just bringing more difficult circumstances to you now. Let it all go, no matter what it is. Do it for you. If you hold a grudge or blame someone for something in the past, you are only harming you." I have often said that one of life's greatest achievements is to let go and let God. If someone else is being blessed, but it appears that we are not at the moment, we should thank the Lord for that person's blessings because that is what will insure that we get blessed. Love is a boomerang – what we throw out will come right back. If we put love into action by sending it out, I declare to you that it will come back. All of what we do and are starts in our minds. Let us not hate others but instead appreciate them. I often tell my congregation, don't hate, celebrate, don't hate appreciate.

'We can destroy ourselves by cynicism and disillusion just as effectively as by bombs.' – Kenneth B. Clark, noted African-American educator and psychologist.

Believe me I know that it is a real challenge to love someone when that person is abusing you, either verbally or physically. And it is extremely difficult to show people love when things are not going as well as you would like them to go on the job, or when your relationships are in tatters or your children have decided they won't listen to you any more. I have found what works is just to keep on loving them, anyway.

Sometimes you literally have to love the hell out of people. When I have done that, God has far exceeded the level of love I sent out with the blessings that He gave me back in return. John Milton said, "The mind is its own place, and in itself can make a heaven of hell, a hell of heaven."

There is a proven way to thwart the devil's attempts to harm relationships among people, particularly between men and women. I am speaking specifically to women here. If your husband stays out longer than you know he should be out, my advice would be do not just sit there waiting for him with rollers in your head and a stick in your hand. You do not look inviting like that. Here is a better strategy to greet your husband when he finally gets home: Prepare something to eat for him, along with his favorite beverage. You might want to say something like, "Hi honey. Boy you look hungry. Would you like something to eat?" He will be caught off guard, and won't know what hit him or where it came from. You will wear down his rebellious spirit with your kindness because it confuses the enemy, who expects us to act just like him. We also must not keep bringing up the sins of the past, if we expect to move into a loving and positive future. I like what Marlene Dietrich, famed actress of the last century, said: "Once a woman has forgiven a man, she must not reheat his sins for breakfast." In other words – think love.

Sometimes you literally have to love hell out of people. When I have done that, God has far exceeded the level of love I sent out with the blessings that He gave me back in return.

REMOVING THE UNNECESSARY

In her book, *Becoming Yourself: The Journey from Head to Heart*, Jan Engels-Smith told the story about a sculptor, who had a large boulder in his possession. The rock was huge in magnitude and the sculptor spent several months chipping away at it. When he finished, it was a beautifully hand-carved elephant. When asked how he created such a magnificent piece of art from what had been such a coarse object, the sculptor replied, "If I want to carve an elephant in stone, I simply chip away all of the stone that does not look like an elephant." I just wonder what would happen if we chipped away at everything that was not love in us so that nothing was left except just that – love. Imagine how much satisfaction we would get if we whittled away everything within us but compassion, so that nothing but compassion was left. Or cut away everything but kindness, so that we became walking kindness. Sometimes we cannot see the forest for the trees. It is the way we think that determines our fate.

'The mind is its own place, and in itself can make a heaven of hell, a hell of heaven.' – John Milton, an English poet, prose polemicist, and civil servant.

What if, just what if, you decided one day to chip away at that thing you have been holding inside of you against uncle or aunt so and so for a long time? Supposing that you began carving away at the guilt that has been bottled up inside of you for something you did years ago that your son or daughter did not appreciate? You say that you had a baby out of wedlock. That was not the right decision, at the time, but you did it. You were not the first and will not be the last woman to be an unwed mother. The baby is here now and must be raised, so chip away at your feelings of shame. So, you have spent some time in prison. Well, sir, welcome to the club. You are not alone – by far. A record 7 million-plus people were behind bars, on probation, or on parole in the U.S. in 2008. If truth be told, some of us just missed being there with you. OK, so you live in a country where you are part of a minority group. That is no reason for you to be down on yourself and have low self-esteem? Chip, chip, chip… Just start chipping away at everything in your past that needs to be diminished. Banish all of those negative thoughts out of there. Chisel away those things that keep you from being the generous, grand and the great person that God intended for you to be. Begin chipping away at all the frustration, foolishness, and flesh – everything that does not look, love, and think like God. Erase, eradicate and evaporate all of those jealous, mean and selfish thoughts.

'Once a woman has forgiven a man, she must not reheat his sins for breakfast.' – Marlene Dietrich, famed 20th century American actress.

Alan Paton wrote this about South Africa's brutal apartheid system in his novel, *Cry, The Beloved Country,* "Help me by love to be a witness of your love." *The tools of our trade aren't for marketing or manipulation, but they are for demolishing that entire massively corrupt culture. We use our powerful God-tools for smashing warped philosophies, tearing down barriers erected against the truth of God, fitting every loose thought and emotion and impulse into the structure of life shaped by Christ* (2 Corinthians 10:4-5).

I wish I could convey to you the depth of how thankful I am that God has chipped away at some of the things in me that did not need to be there, and He is not through with me yet. Everyday He is shaping and reshaping me to look like Him. I thank God for the people in my life who have loved me, in spite of me. This unconditional love coming from the throne of God or from the heart of the human being has the power to set the captive free. Jesus started the chipping process for mankind when He died, on the cross, more than two millennia ago. When the Lord began chipping away at the debt for our sins, the only thing that survived was love. I am talking about love on a cross where Jesus was stretched wide and pierced in the side just for you and me. What an extraordinary love. Now it's our turn. On your mark, get set… go!

Coaching Questions

Chapter One – 'As A Man Thinketh'

1. What are the issues that you most identify with in this chapter?

2. How have people with an errant thought process affected our society?

3. What was James Allen's most famous book about?

4. What does it mean to be made in the Imago Dei?

5. What steps do you need to take to receive the benefits discussed in this chapter?

Chapter Two – A Message From The Trees

1. What are the issues that you most identify with in this chapter?

2. Why do trees need taproots?

3. What causes the bonsai tree to have stunted growth?

4. What did the Indianapolis ministerial group ask for from their political leaders?

5. What steps do you need to take to receive the benefits discussed in this chapter?

Chapter Three – The Burning Bush: Religion vs. Relationship

1. What are the issues that you most identify with in this chapter?

2. Why do you think the burning bush that Moses saw did not burn up?

3. What is the biggest difference that you see between religion and relationship?

4. What percentage of black males are predicted to go to prison over their lifetimes?

5. What steps do you need to take to receive the benefits discussed in this chapter?

Chapter Four – Think Love!

1. What are the issues that you most identify with in this chapter?

2. Giving someone else one of your organs is an example of what?

3. What do people sometimes fail to do while they are at church?

4. What does the acronym EGO stand for?

5. What steps do you need to take to receive the benefits discussed in this chapter?

Chapter Five – Speaking Spirits

1. What are the issues that you most identify with in this chapter?

2. Do you see any benefit from the fact that you were made in the image of God?

3. For what purpose did God create you?

4. Why do you have to be on guard when you worship God?

5. What steps do you need to take to receive the benefits discussed in this chapter?

Chapter Six – Treasure Chest

1. What are the issues that you most identify with in this chapter?

2. What behavior changes can you make when you become treasure?

3. Approximately how many intimate-partner victims are there in the U.S. annually?

4. What lesson about container and content did you learn from the catastrophes in Minneapolis and New Orleans?

5. What steps do you need to take to receive the benefits discussed in this chapter?

Chapter Seven – Renewing Your Mind

1. What are the issues that you most identify with in this chapter?

2. What movie glamorized an urban dance expression called Krumping?

3. Can you name at least one major difference between salvation and sanctification?

4. There is a difference between being present in church and presenting ourselves. What is it?

5. What steps do you need to take to receive the benefits discussed in this chapter?

Chapter Eight – 'Man In The Mirror'

1. What are the issues that you most identify with in this chapter?

2. Can you name one consequence of not understanding your purpose in life?

3. What did God mean when He told us to multiply, subdue and replenish the earth?

4. What did God promise we would receive after we are baptized with the Holy Spirit?

5. What steps do you need to take to receive the benefits discussed in this chapter?

Chapter Nine – The Imago Dei

1. What are the issues that you most identify with in this chapter?

2. How can the Lord be inside and outside of you at the same time?

3. How can the "I AM" power help you to get off of spiritual welfare?

4. If you're a Christian, what reflection should you see in the mirror?

5. What steps do you need to take to receive the benefits discussed in this chapter?

Chapter Ten – Attitude Of Gratitude

1. What are the issues that you most identify with in this chapter?

2. What biblical thesis does the theology of "heaven on earth" support?

3. The phrase "attitude of gratitude" is part of what law?

4. What major industry is bombarding our minds with information?

5. What steps do you need to take to receive the benefits discussed in this chapter?

Chapter Eleven – His Eye Is On The Sparrow

1. What are the issues that you most identify with in this chapter?

2. With billions of people in the world, what assurance is there that God cares for you, personally?

3. What does the term "broken-wing syndrome" describe about someone's life?

4. What was the value of those rusty old nails that were driven into Jesus' hands?

5. What steps do you need to take to receive the benefits discussed in this chapter?

Chapter Twelve – On Your Mark, Get Set, Go...

1. What are the issues that you most identify with in this chapter?

2. Name three personal traits formed in the first 36 months of your life?

3. What kind of foundation are right thinking and loving based upon?

4. What did you learn from the lesson about the sculptor's elephant?

5. What steps do you need to take to receive the benefits discussed in this chapter?

Resource Bibliography

Allen, James, *As A Man Thinketh*, Ilfracombe, England: Fall River Press, 1992

Benjamin, Jr., T. Garrott, *Boys to Men*, Indianapolis, Indiana: Heaven on Earth Publishing House, 1993

Benjamin, Jr., T. Garrott, *The Home Alone Syndrome*, Indianapolis, Indiana: Heaven on Earth Publishing House, 1994

Benjamin, Jr., T. Garrott, *Mama's Boy*, Indianapolis, Indiana: Vision International Publishing, 2002

Byrne, Rhonda, *The Secret*, Melbourne, Australia: Atria Books, 2006

Gaines, Ernest J., *The Autobiography of Miss Jane Pittman*, San Francisco, California: Bantam Books, 1971

Jakes, T. D., *Reposition Yourself: Living Life Without Limits*, Dallas, Texas: Atria Books, 2007

Jordan, E. Bernard, *The Laws of Thinking*, New York, New York: Hay House, Inc., 2006

Lucado, Max, *Next Door Savior*, San Antonio, Texas: Thomas Nelson, 2003

Meyer, Joyce, ***Battlefield of the Mind Devotional***, St. Louis, Missouri: FaithWords, 2006

Rogers, J. A., ***From Superman to Man***, Chicago, Illinois: Amereon Limited, 1957

Rush, Rickie G., ***May I Have Your Order, Please?*** Dallas, Texas: RGR Publishing, 2005

Treat, Casey, ***Renewing the Mind: The Foundation of Your Success***, Seattle, Washington: Harrison House Publishers, 2000

Warren, Rick, ***The Purpose Driven Life***, Lake Forest, California: Zondervan Publishing Company, 2002

Visit www.tombenjamin.com or www.booksurge.com
to order additional copies.

Or write to:

Vision International Publishing
P.O. Box 781344
Indianapolis, IN 46278-1344

Or call:

1-800-847-9695

Published by:

Vision International Publishing
P.O. Box 781344
Indianapolis, IN 46278